Westward

And the wagon trains move... Illinois, across the mighty Mississippi river, through Missouri and ever westward! These Americans came from the East, settling in Louisiana and Texas, while other pioneers trekked through what was to become Arizona, Utah, Montana. On the move. Searching. They crossed the continent to settle the land, to find fortune.

Over 250 thousand pioneers migrated to the west coast in the mid-1800's, enduring the hardships of hostile terrain. Women provided the strength and reason to endure. Their determination to meet the goal and to keep their families intact is documented in their needlework. Wrapping up in a quilt was a home when there was no house. Wrapping up in a quilt was a comfort when there was no medical service. Wrapping up in a quilt was a shroud when there was no graveyard......

Darlene Palmer (standing) and Anne Dease got into the spirit of the occasion and graciously teamed up to sew the Pioneer Sampler featured on the cover.

Within these pages you will discover wonderful quilt blocks, reminders of history and geography that are a part of our American heritage. Twelve traditional and recognizable quilt blocks are offered for your creative pleasure. They finish in the standard twelve inch square size, adaptable for other projects as well as block exchanges. Use the suggested fabric values, or do some pioneering of your own. The amount of yardage offers you some latitude in combining your chosen fabrics in different combinations. But enjoy the freedom to stretch and grow by using fewer or more fabrics. As you explore your own tastes in color, your quilt will evolve as a unique expression of these old and familiar block patterns that capture a part of America.

Eleanor Burns, a quilter whose appreciation of the past leads today's quilters into the future.

Yardage

Yardage

Twelve 12" Blocks   Approximate Finished Size: 57" x 70"

Fabric

Pictured are Marcus Brothers Baltimore Album Quilt Prints designed by Judie Rothermel.

Select good quality 45" wide 100% cotton fabric of similar weight.

Color

Start by selecting two different color families that compliment each other such as red and blue, purple and teal, or peach and green. When choosing your fabrics, lay them together to see which ones go best with all the others.

Each block calls for a light, a dark, and either one or two mediums. Or be creative and plan your own choices of values and number of fabrics. Or be a pioneer and make a scrap quilt!

Light Background

1 ½ yds of one light,
or more than one light to total the same

Choose a light value fabric which appears solid from a distance, or a non-distracting small print. It must be light enough to contrast with the other fabrics. Good choices are muslin, white print on muslin, or white print on white fabric.

Medium and Dark

¾ yd each of 4 to 6 mediums and darks

With your two color families in mind, select at least one dark. Vary the size of the prints, as a large scaled multi-colored print, a medium scaled print, a small scaled print and one that appears solid from a distance. Mediums and darks are interchangeable in the blocks as long as there is the desired contrast.

How much of each fabric to use is determined, not by the instructions, but rather where you decide to use them.

Yardage

Lattice

1 ⅛ yds
Cut (12) 3" x 45" strips
From these,
Cut (3) strips into (8) 3" x 12 ½" strips
Leave (9) uncut

Select a solid color of 100% cotton that coordinates with your two main colors. Consider making the fabric selection after several blocks are completed and can be placed on the choices.

Border

1 ¼ yds
Cut (7) 6" x 45" strips

Any medium or dark in the quilt can be used. Square off the selvage edges and sew the short ends into one long strip. Clip the threads and press the seams to one side. The border strip is ready to be cut to needed widths and lengths for either "finish."

Seminole Patchwork (Optional)

½ yd lattice fabric
½ yd medium or dark fabric
½ yd border fabric
Layer cut right sides together:
(1) 4" x 8" rectangle medium or dark fabric
(1) 4" x 8" rectangle border fabric
Cut:
(5) 2 ½" x 45" strips lattice
(5) 2 ½" x 45" strips medium or dark
(5) 2 ½" x 45" strips border

Use the same fabric selected for the lattice and border so the seminole patchwork appears to float. Any medium or dark used in the quilt that coordinates with the other two can be used.

Backing

3 ½ yds
Cut into (2) equal pieces

Remove the selvages, and sew those edges together. The seam appears horizontally across the center back of the finished quilt.

Bonded Batting

72" x 90"

Select a thick 8 oz bonded batting for a quick turn finish. Select a lightweight 3 oz bonded batting for a machine quilted finish with binding.

Binding (Machine Quilted Finish Only)

⅔ yd
Cut (7) 3" x 45" strips

Square off the selvage edges, assembly-line sew the short ends into one long strip, and clip the threads. Press lengthwise, wrong sides together.

Supplies

Supplies Needed

General Supplies

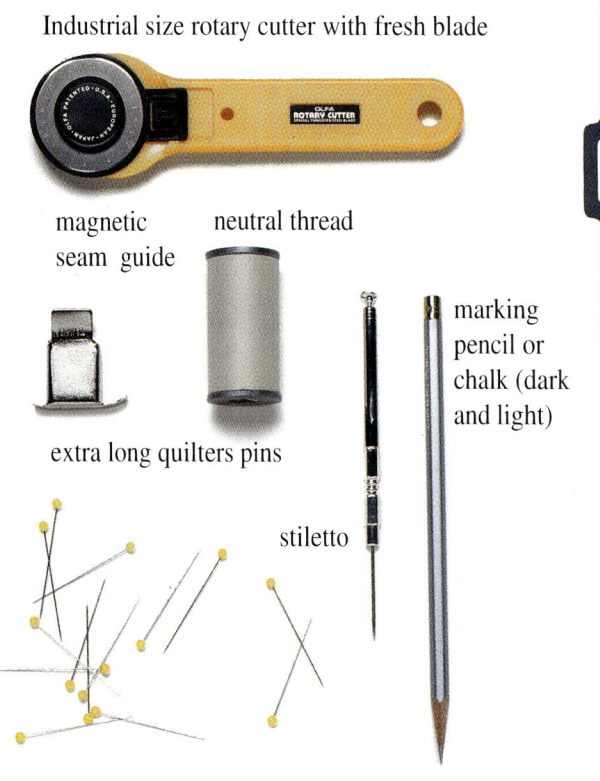

gridded cutting mat

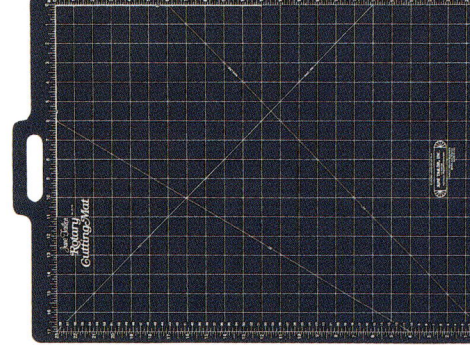

Industrial size rotary cutter with fresh blade

magnetic seam guide

neutral thread

marking pencil or chalk (dark and light)

extra long quilters pins

stiletto

6" x 24" ruler

6" x 6" square ruler

12 ½" Square Up ruler

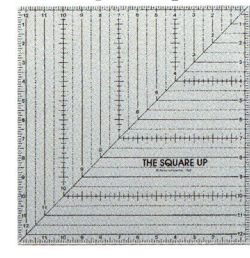

Additional Supplies

For Quilted Finish:
- Nylon filament invisible thread
- Walking foot attachment
- (50) 1" safety pins and a grapefruit spoon or pinning tool to aid pin basting

For Quick Turn Finish:
- Curved needle
- Embroidery floss

How to Use this Book

Color Codes

Several techniques are used throughout the book. Refer to these detailed explanations for these methods.

Cutting Instructions

Instead of cutting out template shapes to construct the block, you are given measurements.

The first page shows a color photograph. The cutting instructions on this page color codes the suggested number of light, medium and dark fabrics to correlate with the photograph. This tells which of your fabrics to cut for specific parts of the block. The small color patches to the right show what the fabric pieces will make once the sewing is completed.

For instance in January:

5" x 10" rectangle light
5" x 10" rectangle dark

Once sewn this . . . . .yields this

Cutting Patches

Select a light and a dark fabric.
Press right sides together with light on top, lining up selvage edges on a corner of the fabric.

With the 12 ½" Square Up ruler, layer cut pieces slightly larger than 5" x 10".

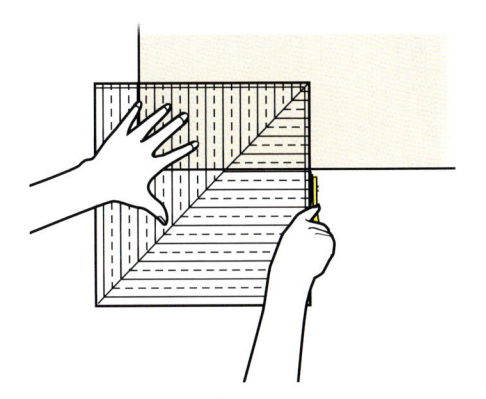

Turn the pieces, and cut to exact size of 5" x 10". Pieces cut right sides together are now ready for sewing instructions on the second page.

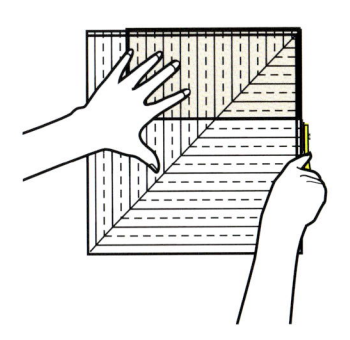

How to Use this Book

Cutting Squares

Use the 6" square ruler for cutting pieces smaller than 6". For several squares, cut a strip that measurement first, and then cut the squares.

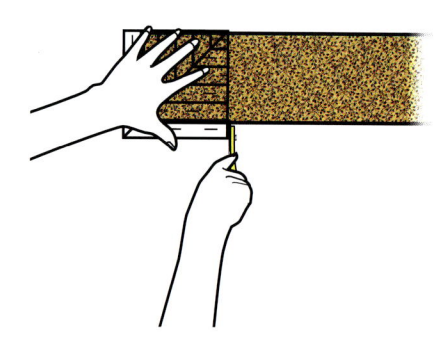

"Fussy Cuts"

To do "fussy cuts," center the design within the square.

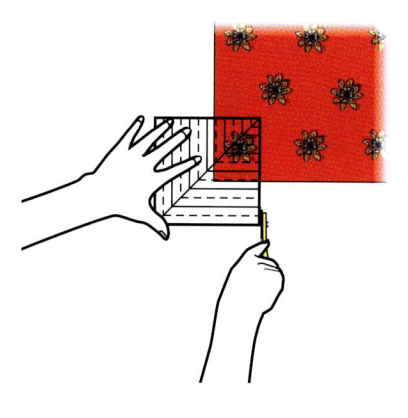

Cutting Strips

When cutting rectangles and squares, cut from one side of the 45" wide fabric. Cut strips from the opposite side of the fabric with the 6" x 24" ruler.

Straighten the edge.
Move your ruler over until the ruler lines are at the newly cut edge.
Carefully and accurately line up and cut the strips at the measurements given.

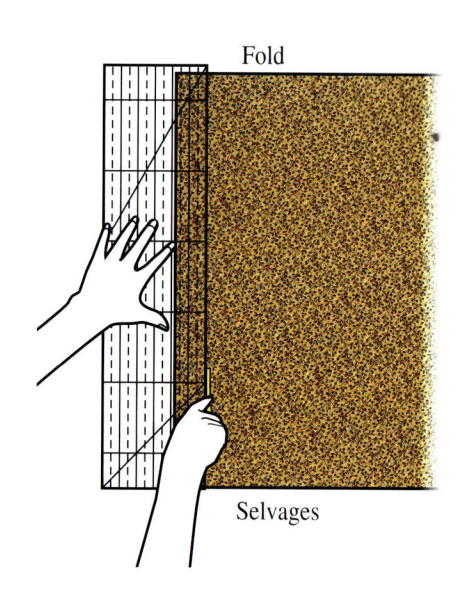

How to Use this Book

Sewing and Pressing Techniques

The next pages give instructions for making the block parts from the pieces just cut. Each patch is color coded to indicate which fabrics to use in the step-by-step directions.

The Grid Method

Patches of two triangles start with two fabrics layered, pressed right sides together, and cut as a square or rectangle.

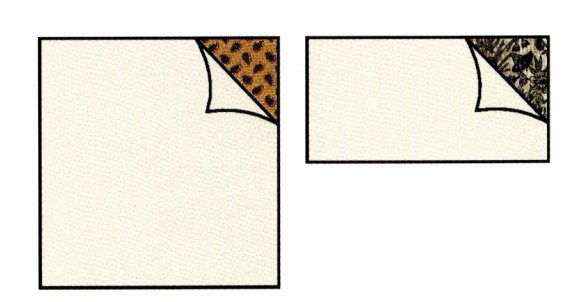

Draw a grid of squares as specified on the wrong side of the layered fabric. Use the lines of the cutting mat to line up the ruler.

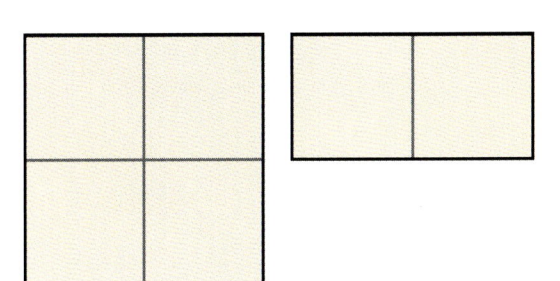

Marking

With a pencil draw diagonal lines across the grid so you can continuously sew ¼" on both sides of the line. Pin.

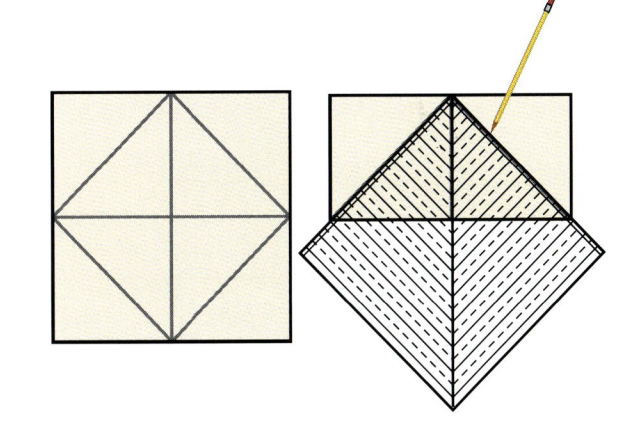

Thread

Use a neutral colored thread. An off-white, gray or light blue thread usually blends with any colors. If you are using a bright white fabric, use white thread.

Stitches per Inch

Use 15 stitches per inch, or 2 to 2.5 on machines with stitch selections from 1 to 4.

7

Sewing

Sew an accurate and consistent ¼" seam allowance. Sew a few stitches ¼" from the diagonal line. Check by measuring between the line and the stitching. If necessary, make adjustments by changing your needle position, or your foot until your seam is ¼". If the presser foot of your machine doesn't give a ¼" seam allowance, there are brands available which might fit your machine, such as Little Foot™ or the Elna quarter inch foot.

Sew a ¼" seam on both sides of the diagonal lines, pivoting with the needle in the fabric. Do not sew on the straight lines.

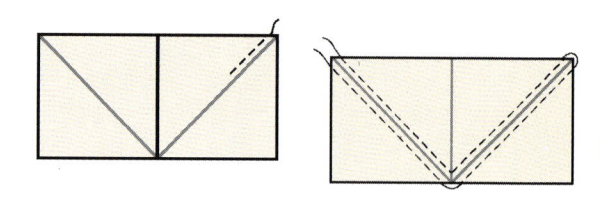

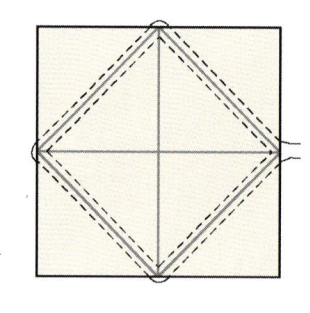

Pressing

Press the sewn grid. Cut on the horizontal and vertical lines, then cut on the diagonals.

Lay the pieces on the ironing board with the darker fabric on top. Open the triangles, pressing the seam allowance to the darker fabric....unless you are directed to press to the lighter fabric for easier construction. Press carefully to avoid leaving folds at seam lines. Using steam is a personal preference.

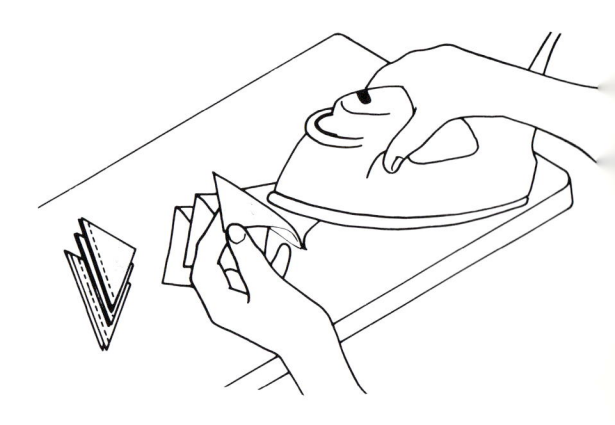

Squaring Up

Trim the oversized patch to the specified size using the 6" square ruler. Lay the ruler's diagonal line on the seam, and trim two edges.
Turn the patch and lay the diagonal line on the seam. Place the ruler lines of the specified measurement on the newly cut edges, and trim the final edges.

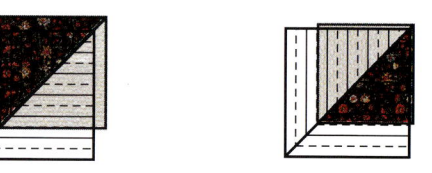

Assembly-line Sewing

Save time and thread when sewing several paired pieces by butting one after another without cutting the thread or removing from the machine.

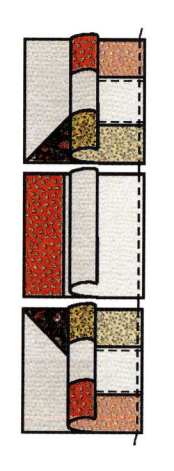

The Triangle Pieced Rectangle Method
(the Flying Geese Patch)

Several blocks have Triangle Pieced Rectangles (TPR's). These finish in different sizes, but the method is the same and produces four identical patches.
(This example is a 7 ¼" square on an 8 ½" square to yield 3 ½" x 6 ½" pieces which finish as 3" x 6" patches.)

1. Right sides together and same grain, exactly center the smaller square on the larger square. To find the "same grain," tug on each square to find the direction of more "give." Press.
2. Draw a diagonal line. Pin.
3. Sew **exactly** ¼" from both sides of line. Press.

4. Cut on line. Press seam allowances toward larger triangles.

5. Place right sides together with opposite fabrics touching. **The seams do not lock.** Match outside edges. Press.
6. Draw a diagonal line across seams. Pin.
7. Sew a ¼" on both sides of line. Press.

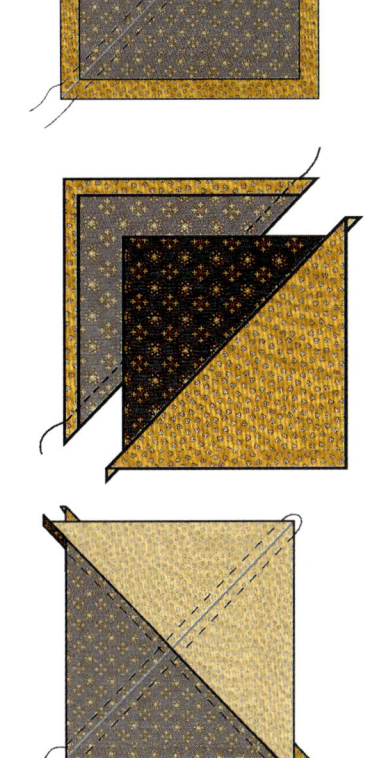

8. Cut on line. On each piece, find the mid-point between seams and clip seam allowance to stitching in order to press seam allowances to larger triangles.

Clip to stitching between seams

9. When trimming out four patches, notice the dimensions given for your block. This example produces patches 3 ½" x 6 ½". It is necessary to center the peak, leave a ¼" seam allowance above it, and make sure the seams end in the corners.

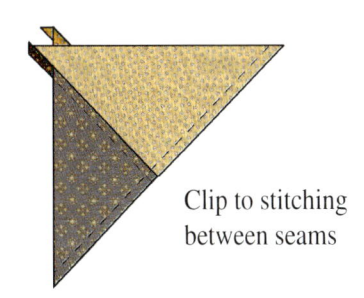

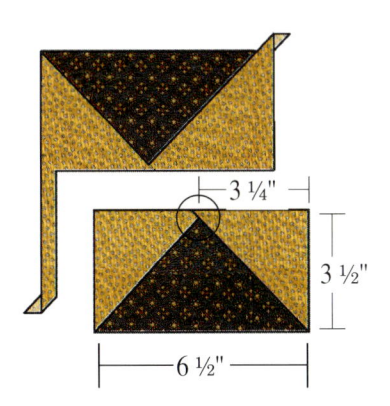

3 ¼"

3 ½"

6 ½"

How to Use this Book

9

January

Golden Gate

Suggested values: choose a light, a dark and two mediums.

The Golden Gate is the strait linking San Francisco Bay with the Pacific Ocean. It is wide and deep enough to accommodate oceangoing vessels.

The Emigrants' Guide to California, by Joseph Ware, estimated the cost of a voyage by ship around the Horn at six hundred dollars per person, compared to the same price of moving a family of four overland by covered wagon.

Guidebooks recommended taking two or three quilts per traveler, which was sufficient bedding to last the trip and several years after arrival.

Cutting Instructions

Layer cut right sides together:

(1) 5" x 10" rectangle light
(1) 5" x 10" rectangle dark

Cut:

(1) 1 ⅞" x 19" strip first medium
(1) 1 ⅞" x 19" strip light
(1) 1 ⅞" x 19" strip second medium

(1) 4 ½" square light or fussycut

To Make These Pieces

4

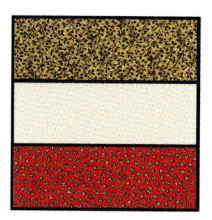

4

1

January

Making Four

1. Press rectangles right sides together.
2. Draw a 5" squaring line.
3. Draw diagonal lines. Pin.
4. Sew ¼" on both sides of diagonal lines. Press.
5. Cut on drawn lines.
6. Press seams toward darker fabric.
7. Square to 4 ½".

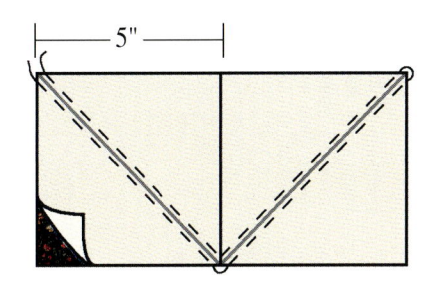

Making Four

1. Sew strips together.
2. Press seams toward darker fabrics. Measure width. If it is more than 4 ½", sliver trim the edges equally.
3. Trim end, and cut four 4 ½" sections.

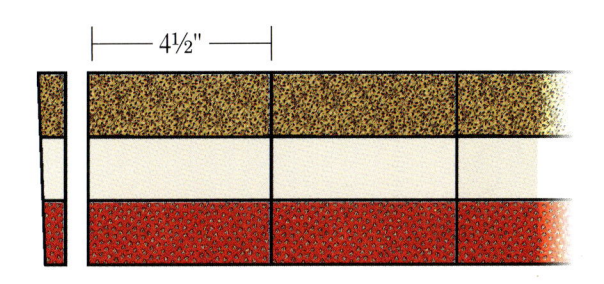

Sewing the Block Together

1. Lay out pieces.
2. Flip middle row onto left row, right sides together.
3. Assembly-line sew vertical seam.
4. Flip right row onto middle row. Sew.
5. Sew horizontal rows, pushing seams in opposite directions and away from center square.
6. Press.

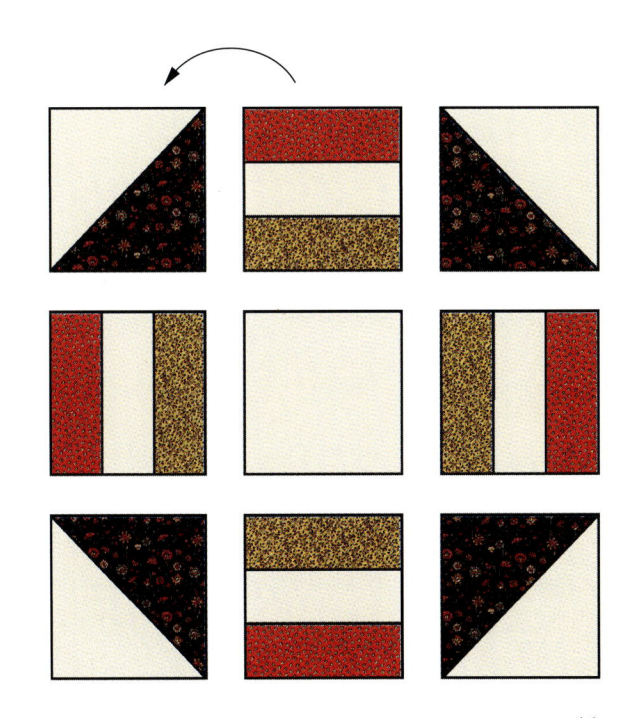

January

Sunday	Monday	Tuesday	Wednesday

San Francisco Fabrics
Vi Hamblett, Owner
Joan Sipherd, Manager
1715 Polk St.
San Francisco, CA 94109
(415) 673-5848

Joan's favorite Quilt in a Day book is the *Amish* because of the graphic quality of the design.
Tip: After a quilt is washed it should be spread flat until dry. If you are short on space, lay a plastic painter's cloth over the bed, spreading the quilt on top to dry. (Joan Sipherd)

January

Thursday	Friday	Saturday

Ratatouille
Joan Sipherd
San Francisco Fabrics

1 lg. onion, chopped coarsely
½ clove fresh garlic, minced
1 bell pepper, cut into squares
¼ c. olive oil
1 lg. eggplant, cut into 1" cubes
2 med. zucchini, sliced into ½" rounds
1 c. fresh mushrooms, whole or sliced
1 15-oz. can stewed tomatoes
1 t. salt
⅛ t. pepper
½ t. basil
½ t. oregano

In a dutch oven or heavy-bottomed saucepan with a lid, saute the onion, garlic, and bell pepper in olive oil until soft; stir in eggplant, zucchini, and mushrooms and saute a few minutes more. Add tomato and seasonings. Cover and simmer gently for about 20 minutes or until all vegetables are well cooked. Uncover and allow liquid to evaporate, to desired consistency and taste; turn up heat if necessary. Variations include addition of a large potato cut in chunks, and carrot rounds. Serves 4-6.

February

Rocky Mountain Puzzle

Suggested values: choose a light, a dark and two mediums.

Cutting Instructions

Layer cut right sides together:

(1) 8" x 8" square light
(1) 8" x 8" square dark

(1) 4" square light
(1) 4" square dark

Cut for "Log Cabin" center:

(1) 3 ½" square first medium or fussycut
(1) 2" x 22" strip second medium

Cut:

(2) 3 ½" squares light

The discovery of gold in 1858 brought explorers to the Rockies, a rugged mountain range that extends over 3,000 miles. Between 1840 and 1870, a quarter of a million Americans crossed those mountains.

The theme of migration is evident in the triangle pieces of the block, often used to represent birds, mountains, waves, or directional movement. Other patterns were Delectable Mountains, Wandering Foot, and Kansas Troubles.

To Make These Pieces

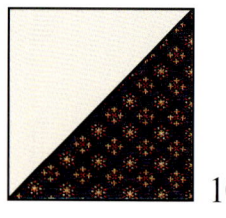

10

1

2

February

Making Ten

1. Press squares right sides together.
2. Draw 4" squaring lines.
3. Method detail on page 7.
4. Square to 3 ½".

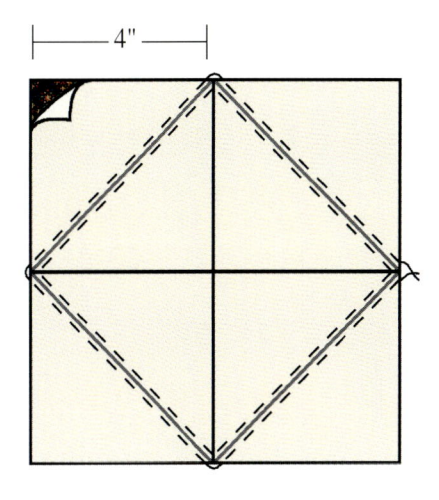

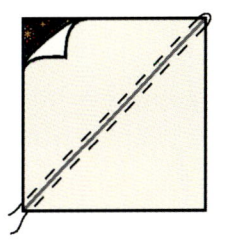

Making the Center

1. Lay center square right sides together on strip. Sew.
2. Trim strip to 3 ½" size of center square. Press seam toward strip fabric.

3. Lay square right sides together on strip. Sew.
4. Trim strip to square-and-strip size, about 5". Press seam toward strip fabric.

5. Lay square right sides together on strip. Sew.
6. Trim, and press seam toward strip fabric.

7. Sew strip to final side. Press seam toward strip fabric.
8. Square to 6 ½".

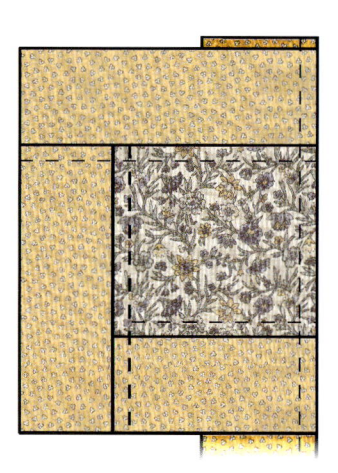

February

Sewing the Block Together

1. Assembly-line sew top and bottom rows. Clip connecting threads.

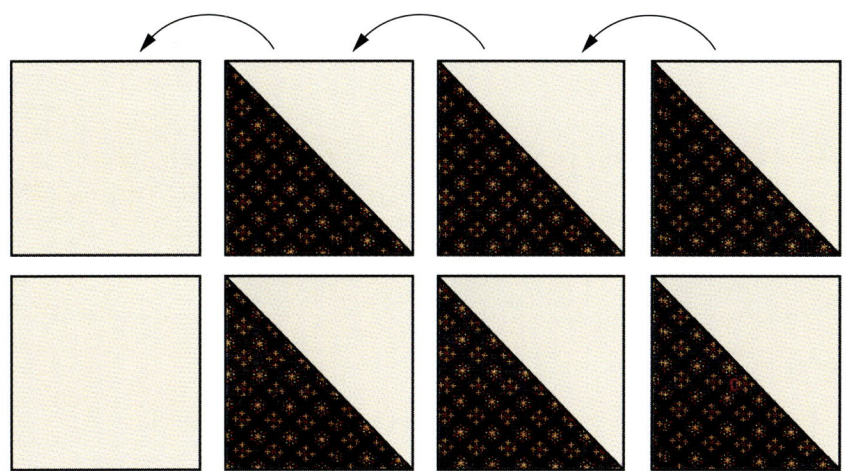

2. Sew side pieces together. Press seams toward dark fabric.

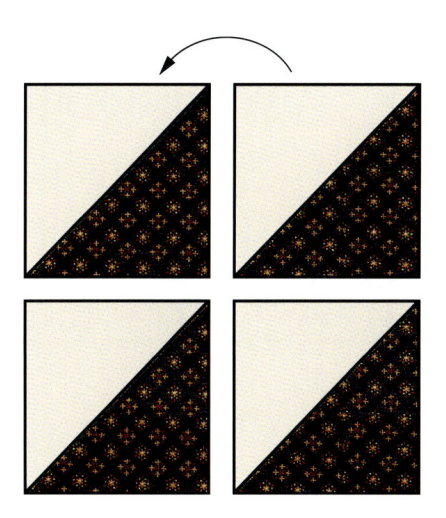

3. Carefully match, pin and sew side pieces to center square. Press seams toward center.
4. Sew top and bottom rows to center row.
5. Press.

17

February

February

Sunday	Monday	Tuesday	Wednesda

February

Quilt Works
Margaret Prina & Shirley Brabson
11117 Menaul NE
Albuquerque, NM 87112
(505) 298-8210

Shirley's favorite Quilt in a Day book is *Sunbonnet Sue* because it is such a popular quilt. Sunbonnet Sue looks great in those reproduction 1930's fabrics.
Tip: Don't be afraid to let your creativity run loose.
(Shirley Brabson)

Thursday	Friday	Saturday

Sour Cream Enchilada Casserole

Shirley Brabson, Quilt Works
Albuquerque, NM

1 can cream of mushroom soup
1 can cream of chicken soup
2 cs. sour cream
8 oz. grated sharp cheddar cheese
1 large onion, minced
green chilies to taste
1 small can mushrooms drained
3-4 cups shredded turkey or chicken
¼ t. cumin
salt & pepper to taste
12 corn tortillas lightly fried in oil & drained

Mix all ingredients except tortillas, saving some cheese for top. Layer mixture with tortillas, top with grated cheese. Bake at 350° F., 30-40 min., 10-12 servings.

March
Chisholm Trail

Jesse Chisholm, an Indian trader, first traveled from San Antonio, Texas, north to Abilene, Kansas, by wagon in 1866. The next year, cattle ranchers drove their herds north, following Chisholm's wheel ruts, through Indian territory in Oklahoma to railroad points in Kansas. Traffic peaked in 1871 with 600,000 cattle.

Unlike the easy swing of the classic song, *The Old Chisholm Trail*, the cowboy had plenty of troubles with weather, food, his boss, and pay.

Suggested values: choose a light, a dark and two mediums.

Cutting Instructions

Layer cut right sides together:

(1) 8" x 8" square light
(1) 8" x 8" square first medium

(1) 4" x 8" rectangle light
(1) 4" x 8" rectangle second medium

(1) 4" square light
(1) 4" square dark

Cut:

(2) 3 ½" squares dark

To Make These Pieces

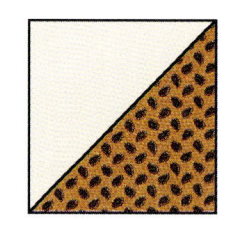

8

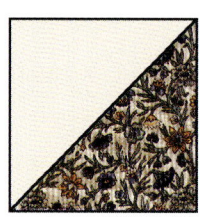

4

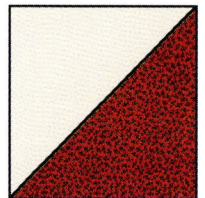

2

2

March

Making Eight

1. Press each paired square and paired rectangle right sides together.
2. Draw 4" squaring lines.
3. Method detail on page 7.
4. Square to 3 ½".

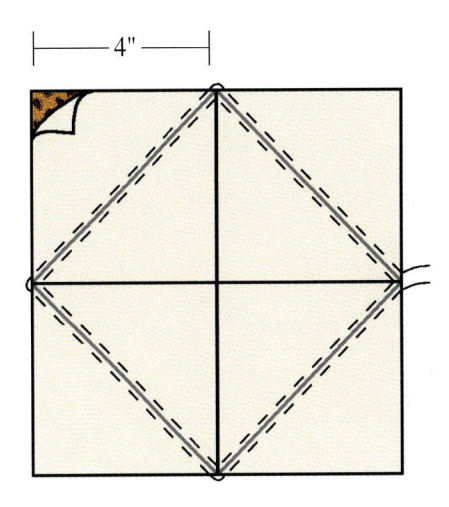

and Four

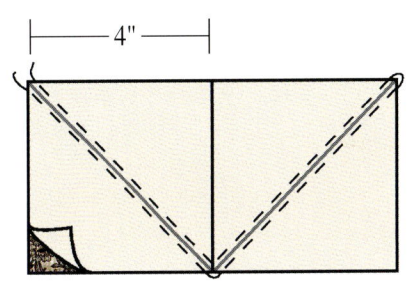

and Two

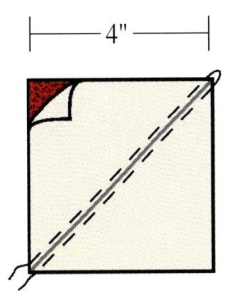

Making Two Quarters

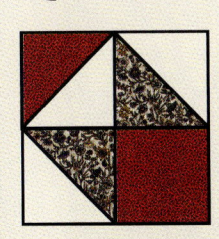

1. Lay out 3 ½" dark squares, light/dark patches and light/second medium patches in piles of two.
2. Flip pieces on right onto pieces on left, and assembly-line sew vertical seam.
3. Assembly-line sew second identical Quarter.
4. Sew horizontal seam of each Quarter.
5. Press. Each Quarter should measure 6 ½" square.

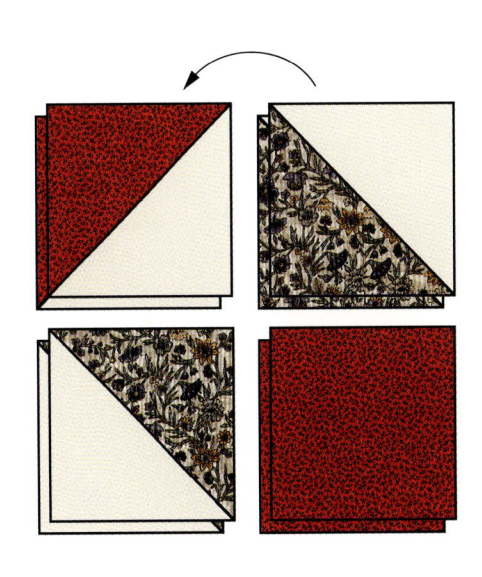

March

Making Two Quarters

1. Lay out light/first medium patches in piles of two.
2. Flip pieces on right onto pieces on left, and assembly-line sew vertical seam.
3. Assembly-line sew second identical Quarter.
4. Sew horizontal seam of each Quarter.
5. Press. Each Quarter should measure 6 ½" square.

Sewing the Block Together

1. Lay out Quarters
2. Flip right Quarters onto left Quarters, and assembly-line sew vertical seam.
3. Sew horizontal rows, pushing vertical seams in opposite directions.
4. Press.

Chisholm Trail is the third block in the first row. Sew together the first row. Turn to the back of Pioneer Sampler for instructions.

These nine Golden Gate blocks are set together without lattice and use only two fabrics—a light and a gold touched oriental print. Four blocks are made with the light fabric as a background, and the remaining five blocks reverse the fabric positions for a positive/negative look. The gold in the oriental flavored fabric is picked up in a gold thread, machine stitched 1/4" from the seams. It is framed in an ocean wave blue, and the binding is the gold fabric.

22

This Rocky Mountain Puzzle quilt has four identical blocks turned in the same direction. The blocks are framed with a lattice and cornerstone setting. The patches and block edges are machine quilted "in the ditch" with invisible thread. The dark fabric is picked up in the border. The center patch fabric is also the binding.

Sixteen identical Rocky Mountain Puzzle blocks set together in alternating directions form a dramatic overall pattern. A secondary pattern emerges where the blocks meet. The value placement changes the look of the block and contributes to the secondary pattern. The quilt is framed in a narrow dark border followed by a wider medium border and finally a wide 1" border binding of the dark fabric. Invisible thread is used to machine "stitch in the ditch."

Four identical Chisholm Trail blocks set together without lattice are planned so that the values and fabrics form a medallion Ohio Star. The star points fabric is repeated in the narrow framing border, while the other borders repeat the main medium and dark fabrics. The last border fabric is also the binding fabric. The quilt is machine quilted "in the ditch" diagonally in both directions with invisible thread .

Four identical Chisholm Trail blocks set together without lattice take on a completely different look with the use of a stripe fabric, changing the value placement, and carrying the pattern into the medium border. A second dark border fabric is repeated in the binding. The quilt is machine quilted "in the ditch" with invisible thread.

March

Sunday	Monday	Tuesday	Wednesday

March

Prairie Quilts, Inc.

Cynthia Houser
5614 E. Lincoln
Wichita, KS 67218
(316) 682-8826

Cynthia likes all of the Quilt in a Day books, but she especially likes the *Log Cabin*. It is the bible of strip piecing and has so many variations. Everyone makes the same pattern but they all look different. **Tip:** Use discretion when choosing batting for machine quilting—it should be thin and firm. Also, be careful to cut batting accurately when cutting it into strips. (Toni de la Garza, Apply Valley, CA)

Thursday	Friday	Saturday

Barbecued Brisket
Cynthia Houser,

6 lb. brisket, sprinkle with 3 T. liquid smoke, garlic powder, onion salt and celery salt. Allow to stand overnight covered with foil. Next morning, sprinkle with pepper and worcestershire sauce. Cover and bake 5 hours at 275° F. Drain grease often. Uncover and bake 1 hour with barbecue sauce.
Boil 15 minutes

Barbecue Sauce:
1 c. catsup
1 t. salt
1 t. celery seed
¼ c. brown sugar
½ c. worcestershire sauce
2 c. water
1 onion, chopped

Texas Sheet Cake
Barbara Wynne, Del Mar, CA

Preheat oven to 350° F.
Combine and sift into mixing bowl:
   2 c. flour
   2 c. sugar
   1 t. cinnamon
   2 t. baking soda
Combine in glass measuring cup & bring to boil in microwave (3 min.)
   2 sticks margarine
   2 T. cocoa
   1 c. water
Pour mixture over above dry mixture, beat to combine.
Add:
   2 eggs
   ½ c. buttermilk
   1 t. vanilla
Beat well to combine.
Bake at 350° F for 15-20 min. in a 12" x 18" cookie sheet with sides or jelly roll pan sprayed with Pam.
Frosting
Bring to a boil:
   1 stick margarine
   4 T. cocoa
Remove from heat and add:
   4 T. buttermilk
   1 box powdered sugar
   ½ c. nuts (optional)

April

Louisiana

Suggested values: choose a light, a dark and a medium.

By 1860, the population of Louisiana exceeded 700,000, and a class system based on plantations with slave labor had developed. Plantation grown crops included indigo, rice, and tobacco. Indigo-blue became a popular dye for quilt fabrics because of its colorfastness.

Determined to establish themselves outside the confines of slavery, many blacks began to emigrate west in the 1840's, while even greater numbers came after the Civil War.

The wheel in the block gives a sense of movement as in slow-moving wagons and by the blowing wind.

Cutting Instructions

Cut:

(1) 7 ¼" square dark
(1) 8 ½" square medium

Layer cut:

(4) 3 ½" x 6 ½" rectangles light

To Make These Pieces

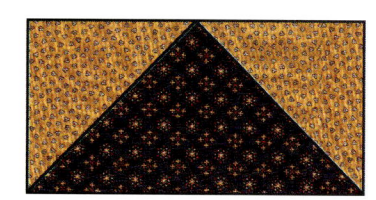

4

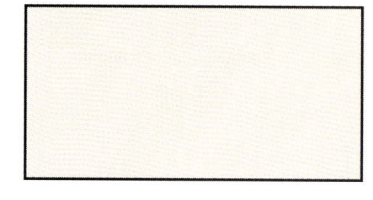

4

April

Making Four

See page 9 for detailed method.

1. Right sides together and same grain, center 7 ¼" square on 8 ½" square. Press.
2. Draw a diagonal line. Pin.
3. Sew ¼" both sides of line. Press.

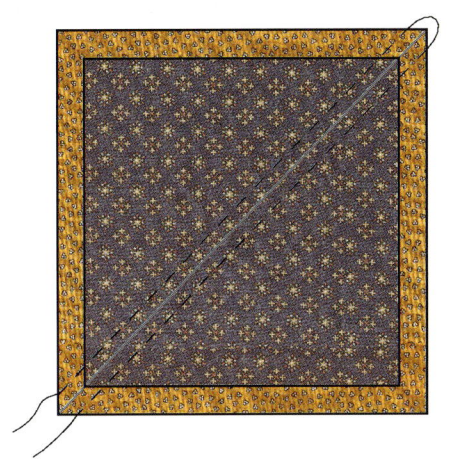

4. Cut on line. Press seam allowances toward larger triangles.

5. Place right sides together with opposite fabrics touching. **The seams do not lock**. Match outside edges. Press.
6. Draw a diagonal line across seams. Pin.
7. Sew a ¼" on both sides of line. Press.

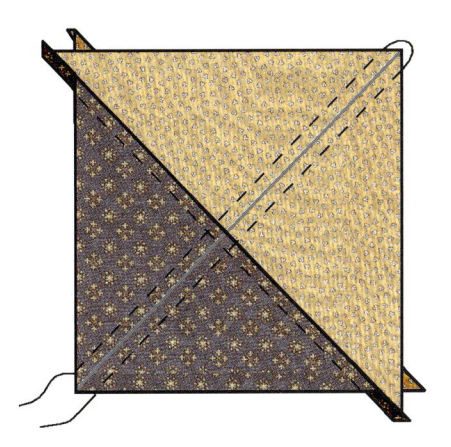

8. Cut on line. On each piece, find the mid-point between the seams and clip seam allowance to stitching in order to press seam allowances to larger triangles.

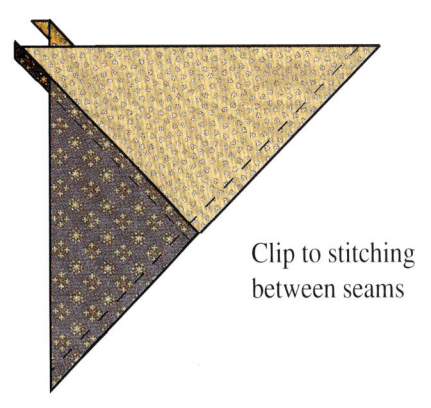

Clip to stitching between seams

9. When trimming out four 3 ½" x 6 ½" patches, center peak at 3 ¼". Leave a ¼" seam allowance above peak. Seams end at bottom corners.

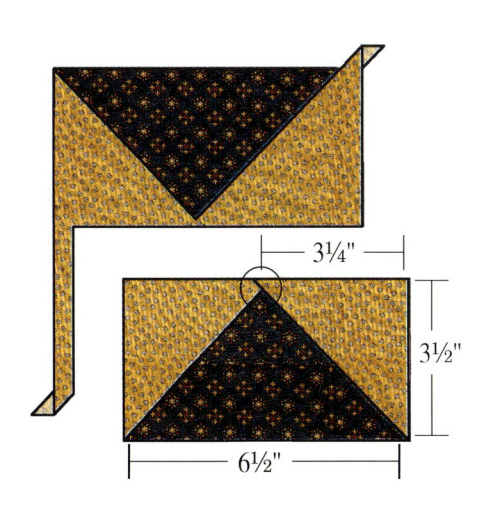

3¼"

3½"

6½"

27

April

Making the Quarters

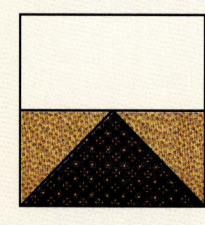

1. Lay out light rectangles with patches.

2. Flip patch onto rectangle, matching outside edges. Sew a ¼" seam across the peak.

3. Assembly-line sew remaining Quarters.

4. Press seams toward rectangle.

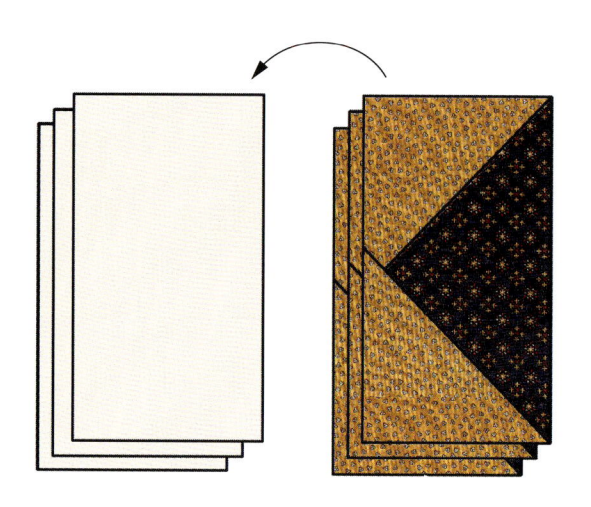

Sewing the Block Together

1. Lay out Quarters.

2. Flip right Quarters onto left Quarters, and assembly-line sew vertical seam.

3. Sew horizontal rows, pushing vertical seams in opposite directions.

4. Press.

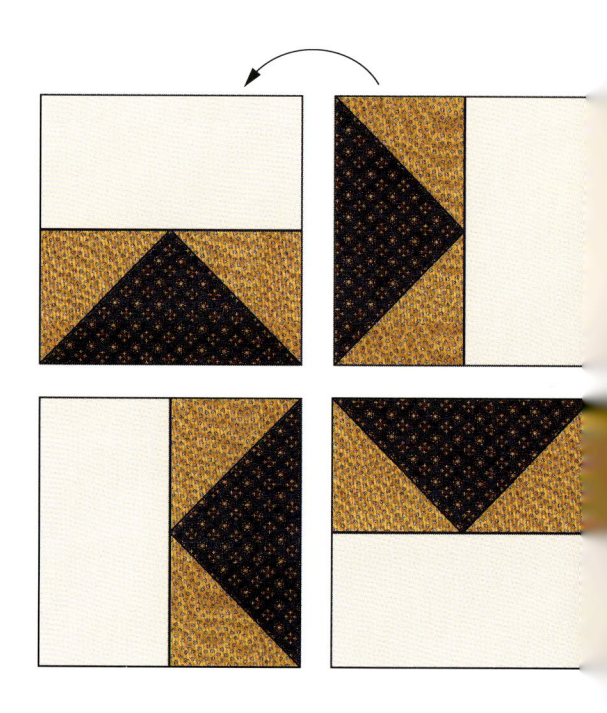

Louisiana takes on a "scrappy" look when 12 blocks are made in different fabrics. They are set together without lattice. In each block the dark print reads solid from a distance, and the medium fabrics are all small prints. The blocks have the same light background in a muslin print. A different dark print is used in the border, while the binding is a solid. The blocks are machine quilted by "stitching in the ditch" with invisible thread.

Four Louisiana blocks in bold fabrics are framed in black lattice with focal point cornerstones. The block background is repeated in the binding. The patches, lattice and cornerstone seams are machine quilted "in the ditch" with invisible thread.

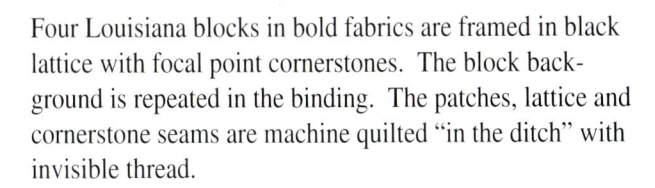

Four Louisiana blocks in medium and lighter fabrics set together with medium solid give this small quilt a delicate, pastel look. The binding is the same as the lattice fabric. Invisible thread is used to machine "stitch in the ditch."

April

April

Sunday	Monday	Tuesday	Wednesday

April

Ginger's Needleworks

Ginger Moore
905 E. Gloria Switch Rd.
Lafayette, LA 70507
(318) 232-7847

Ginger has been in business since 1962. She thinks the easy directions in Quilt in a Day books are great. Her favorite is *Morning Star*.
Tip: If your rotary cutter seems dull, try this tip. Open the cutter, clean the blade, and all parts with a soft cloth. Put a drop of sewing machine oil on both sides of the blade and put back into the cutter. This may help and you may not need a new blade just yet. The first cut should be made on a scrap of old fabric. (Ginger Moore)

Thursday	Friday	Saturday

Shrimp Stew

Ginger Moore
Ginger's Needlework

⅔ c. cooking oil
⅔ c. flour
1 med. onion chopped fine
1 stalk celery chopped fine
½ c. chopped bell peppers
2 to 3 pound peeled shrimp
3 to 4 c. water
salt, black pepper and red pepper to taste

In a heavy skillet with high sides, brown flour in cooking oil over medium heat, stirring constantly to make a roux. When roux is a dark brown color add onions, celery, and bell peppers and stir constantly until they are wilted. Add shrimp still stirring, until they turn pink. Add 3 cups of water, season with salt and pepper to taste. We like it a little spicy. Simmer covered for 45 minutes, check frequently to make sure water does not cook out. Add water, if necessary, to just cover the shrimp when stew is cooked. Serve over steaming hot rice and enjoy.

May

Cheyenne

Suggested values: choose a light, a dark and a medium.

Cheyenne, named after a tribe of Algonquian speaking Indians, became the capital of Wyoming Territory in 1869. It was a shipping point for livestock and a supply center for gold mining in the Black Hills. The town was notoriously lawless until vigilantes imposed order.

Had there been more communication, Native Americans could have assisted the homesteaders avoid starvation and poor nutrition. Indian women knew just the right wild foods to eat, and where to find them. Buried amid tales of fear and misunderstanding, there were tales of compassion between the Indians and the settlers.

Cutting Instructions

Layer cut right sides together:

(1) 4" square light
(1) 4" square medium

(1) 4" square light
(1) 4" square dark

(1) 3 ½" x 14 ½" strip dark
(1) 3 ½" x 14 ½" strip medium

Cut:

(1) 4" square dark, then cut on diagonal
(1) 4" square medium, then cut on diagonal

(1) 4 ¾" square light or fussycut

To Make These Pieces

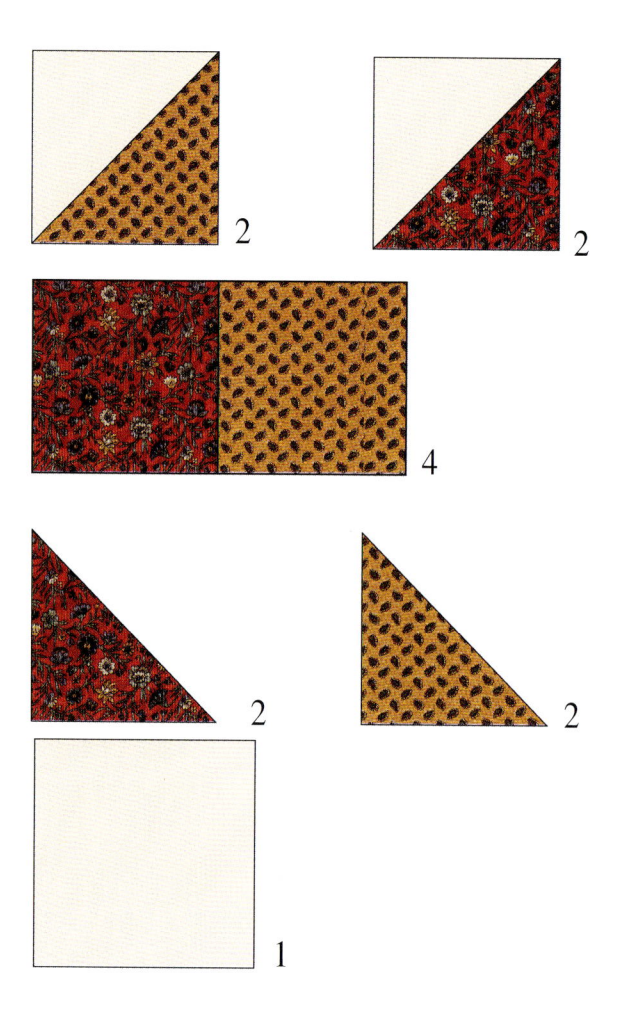

May

Making Two and

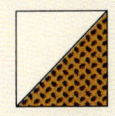

Two

1. Press each paired square right sides together.
2. Draw diagonal lines. Pin.
3. Method detail on page 7.
4. Square to 3 ½".

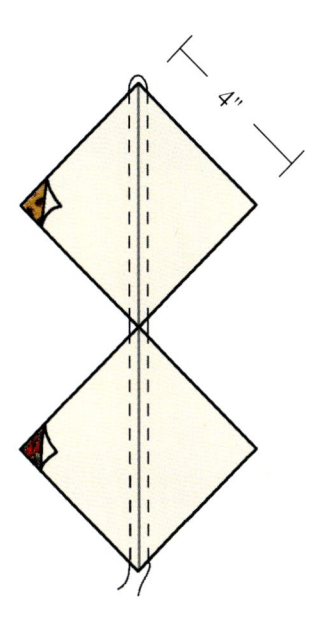

Making the Center

1. Lay out Center square with dark and medium triangles.

2. Flip and pin dark triangles onto square, allowing triangle tips to show evenly. Sew with triangle on bottom.

3. Press seams toward triangles.

4. Add medium triangles, and press seams toward triangles.

5. Square to 6 ½", centering points at 3 ¼". Leave a ¼" seam allowance beyond points.

33

May

Making Four

1. Press and sew strips right sides together.
2. Press seam toward darker fabric.
3. Trim end, and cut four 3 ½" pieces.

Sewing the Block Together

1. Lay out pieces.
2. Flip middle row onto left row, right sides together.
3. Assembly-line sew vertical seam.
4. Flip right row onto middle row. Sew.
5. Sew the horizontal rows, pushing seams in opposite directions.
6. Press.

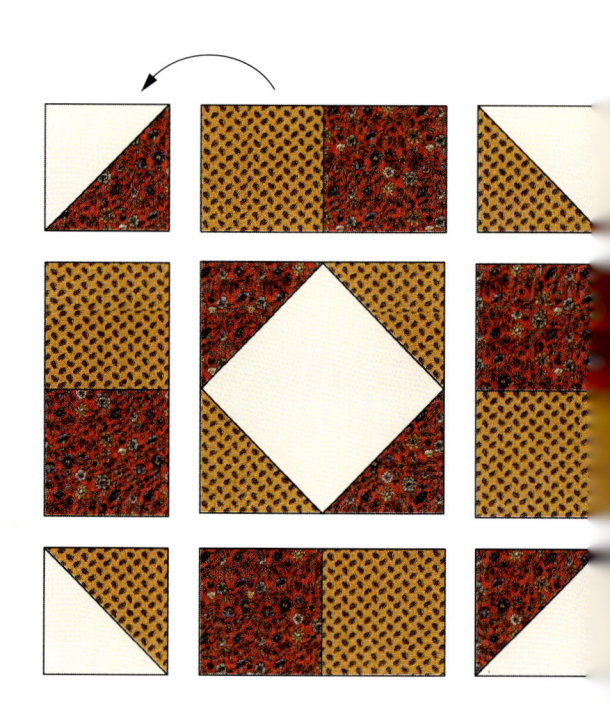

34

Four identical Cheyenne blocks with mainly medium and dark fabrics are set together with a light lattice to lighten the quilt. The dark cornerstones pick up the dark fabric in the block, while the center multi-colored floral of the blocks is repeated in the binding. Machine quilting with invisible thread "in the ditch" completes the quilt.

Fill buckets with river water at night, so the sand settles by morning. Or put a little sweet milk in the water, and it settles in a few minutes.

The journey is long and tiresome. If you can keep the health, the continual occurrence of new objects will make the time pass along more agreeably.

C. C. Parrish
November 15, 1850

Those who come this journey should have their pillows covered with dark calico and sheets colored, white is not suitable.

Charlotte Stearns Pengra
May 18, 1853

May

May

Sunday	Monday	Tuesday	Wednesday

Spencer's Fabrics
Marie Bartley
314 S. Second St.
Laramie, WY 82070
(307) 742-6156

Marie has been in business for 36 years. Her favorite Quilt in a Day book is *Log Cabin*. She says that the *Radiant Star* is very beautiful. Marie shares about Quilt in a Day books "If you can read at all you can make a quilt."
Tip: Have extra bobbins already filled with the thread you are sewing with. (Frances V. Bisner, San Diego, CA)

May

Thursday	Friday	Saturday

Wild Bill's Pinto Bean Chili

Jacalyn Wood, Carlsbad, CA

Recipe adapted from a family recipe from Jacalyn's great grandmother who was born on Buffalo Bill Cody's Ranch.

- **2 pounds of dried pinto beans**
- **2 medium tomatoes chopped or 16 oz can chopped tomatoes**
- **1 ½ tablespoons cumin**
- **1 tablespoon coriander**
- **⅓ cup chili powder (I use New Mexico chili which is extra hot)**
- **3 large cloves garlic minced**
- **1 green pepper chopped fine**
- **1 large red onion chopped fine**
- **1 ½ pounds of lean beef sirloin or lean pork tenderloin, depending on your preference**
- **Salt to taste**
- **Optional:**
- **1 red pepper**
- **1 serrano or jalapeno chili** *(add depending on the spicy flavor you like)*

Place beans in large heavy saucepan or dutch oven and cover with water and bring to a boil. Turn heat down and simmer for 15 minutes. Drain. Return beans to the pan and cover with water by 2". Add all the remaining ingredients except the Meat and Salt. Bring mixture back to a boil. After the beans have reached boiling, turn heat down to simmer. Saute meat until browned. Add to the bean mixture. Cook until the beans are soft, stirring occasionally and making sure that the beans have enough water and do not dry out. Cook about 3-4 hours. Uncover if the beans get too "soupy." Add salt to taste. Beans are best if you let them cool, chill overnight, and then reheat the next day. Garnish with shredded jack or cheddar cheese and cilantro. Serve with fresh flour tortillas and your favorite salsa.

June

Colorado

Suggested values: choose a light, a dark and a medium.

Colorado, Spanish for "reddish," received its first permanent modern settlement in 1858, following the discovery of gold. Mining camps such as Central City and Boulder sprang into existence.

Women came prepared to do their sewing on the trip. It was natural that they pieced or appliqued while on the slow moving wagons, or when sharing the evening with others. A "housewife," a holder for personal items and needlework tools, was often sewn to the lining of a wagon. A gourd held yarn as a woman knitted.

Cutting Instructions

Cut:

(1) 7 ¼" square dark
(1) 8 ½" square light

(4) 3 ½" x 6 ½" rectangles medium

(8) 3 ½" squares light
   do not cut on diagonal

To Make These Pieces

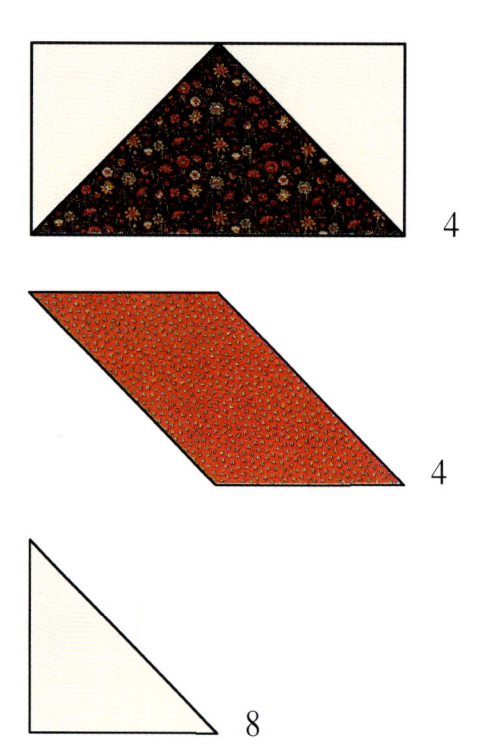

4

4

8

38

Making Four

1. Right sides together and same grain, center 7 ¼" square on 8 ½" square. Press.
2. Method detail on page 9.

3. When trimming out four 3 ½" x 6 ½" patches, center peak at 3 ¼". Leave a ¼" seam allowance above peak. Seams end at bottom corners.

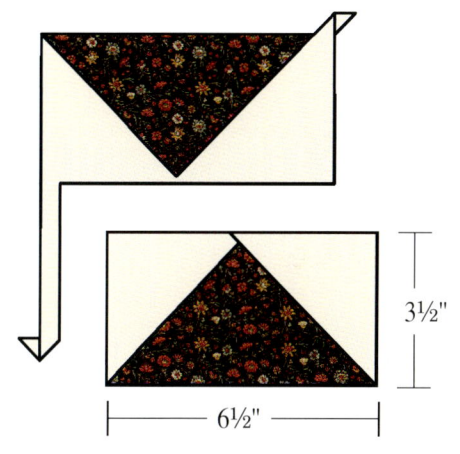

Making Four

1. Draw a diagonal line across the wrong side of each square. To compensate for the fold, lay the ruler from corner to corner so the pencil line will be slightly to the right.
2. Right sides together, press and pin a square to right end of a rectangle.
3. **Sew on diagonal line**. Do not remove from machine. Assembly-line sew remaining rectangles/squares.

4. Measure ¼" from stitches, and trim excess.
5. Press seam toward rectangle fabric.

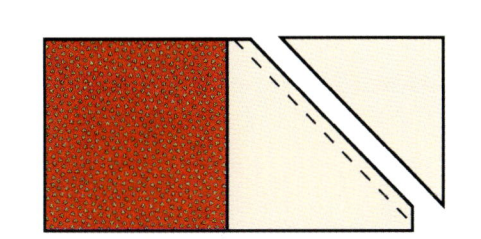

6. Assembly-line sew remaining squares to other edge of rectangles.
7. Trim excess. Press seam toward rectangle fabric.
8. Trim to 3 ½" x 6 ½" with the seams ending at the corners.

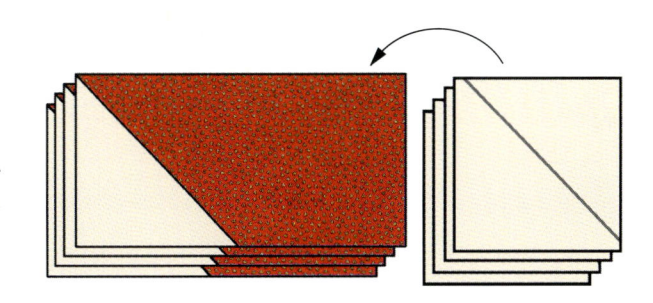

June

Making the Quarters

1. Lay out patches in piles of four.

2. Flip right patch onto left patch. Match the outside edges. Sew.

3. Press seams to triangle.

4. Quarters should measure 6 ½" square.

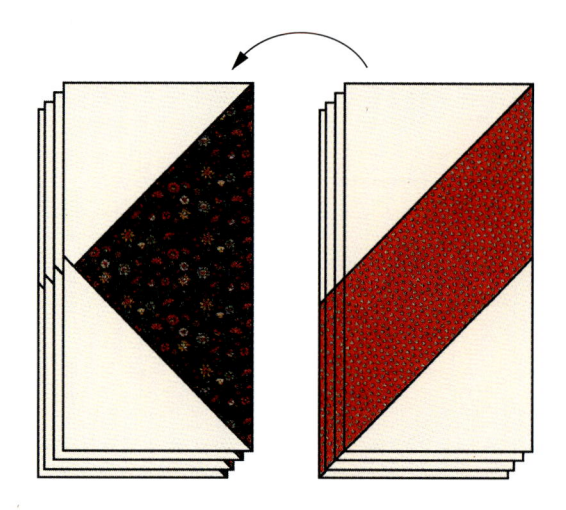

Sewing the Block Together

1. Lay out Quarters.

2. Flip right Quarters onto left Quarters, and assembly-line sew vertical seam.

3. Sew horizontal rows, pushing vertical seams in opposite directions.

4. Press.

Colorado is the third block in the second row. Sew together the second row. Turn to the back of Pioneer Sampler for instructions.

Five identical Colorado blocks and four other identical Colorado blocks in complimentary colors are set together with a solid lattice and no cornerstones. Because this is a fast "quick turn" finish with no additional border, the backing fabric is the same as the lattice fabric. The quilt will be tied rather than machine quilted, and there is no binding. The batting for a tied quilt is thicker than the thin batting used for machine quilting.

Stain Remedies

Grass Stains Molasses
Iron Rust Equal parts of peroxide of hydrogen and household ammonia, or, if there is sunshine - lemon and salt.
Fruit Stains Boiling water poured through the stain before washing.

A piece of magnesia may be kept in a convenient place for use in the temporary concealment of a stain when the dress can not be changed at once.

Thanks to Barbara Gerichs for sharing these tips with us from a cookbook entitled *The Ladies Aid of the M.E. Church*, Lerna, IL (c.1900).

June

Sunday	Monday	Tuesday	Wednesday

The Creative Needle
Marge Serck
6905 S. Broadway #113
Littleton, CO 80122
(303) 794-7312

2553 So. Colorado Blvd.
Denver, CO 80222
(303) 692-8115

Marge said that her favorite Quilt in a Day book is *Sunbonnet Sue Visits Quilt in a Day*.
Tip: For better control of your rotary cutter, place your index finger on the ridge above the blade area. (Janet Lyles)

June

Thursday	Friday	Saturday

Colorado Peach Butter

Janet Lyles, The Creative Needle Littleton, CO

Peel, pit and mash very ripe, even bruised peaches—Colorado Elberta peaches are best. For every cup of pulp, add a cup of sugar, stir well. In a heavy kettle, on very low heat, simmer, stirring frequently, until desired thickness is reached. This may take 8 to 10 hours, just enough time to make your Quilt in a Day. Pour into jars and seal.

P. S. Save the peach pits, soak them in water and simmer for 20 to 30 minutes, strain, add a little red food coloring and use the juice with your favorite pectin to make peach pit jelly.

July
Illinois

Suggested values: choose a light, a dark and two mediums.

Life on the trail was sometimes monotonous. Other times, the pioneers faced death of a loved one, accidents from run-away wagons or stampeding herds, complications of pregnancy and birth, and rapid change in the weather.

To ease the load of starving oxen, possessions were abandoned. When forced to leave behind some of her cargo, one woman wrote a note inviting the next travelers to help themselves to "five good quilts."

Cutting Instructions

Layer cut right sides together:

(1) 5" x 10" rectangle light
(1) 5" x 10" rectangle dark

Cut:

(1) 6 ½" square light
(1) 5 ¼" square dark

(1) 6 ½" square light
(1) 5 ¼" square first medium

(2) 3 ¼" squares light, then cut on diagonal

(1) 3 ⅜" square second medium or fussycut

To Make These Pieces

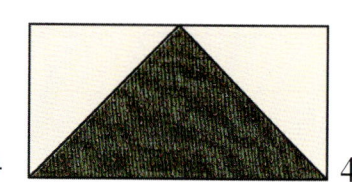

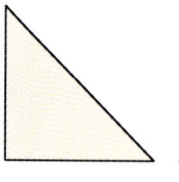

4

4   4

4

1

July

Making Four

1. Press rectangles right sides together.
2. Draw a 5" squaring line.
3. Method detail on page 7.
4. Square to 4 ½".

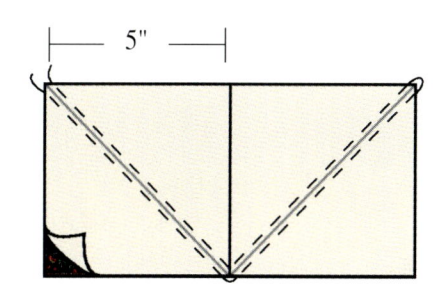

Making Four and Four

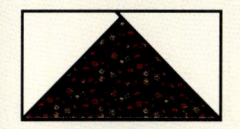

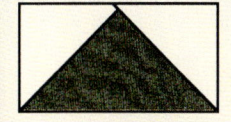

1. Right sides together and same grain, center 5 ¼" squares on 6 ½" squares. Press.
2. Method detail on page 9.

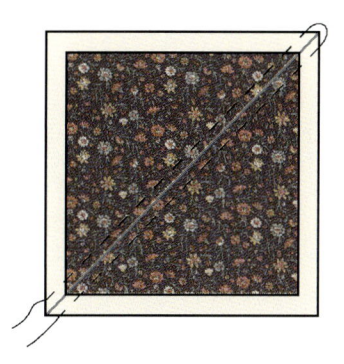

3. When trimming out four 2 ½" x 4 ½" patches, center peak at 2 ¼". Leave a ¼" seam allowance above peak. Seams end at bottom corners.

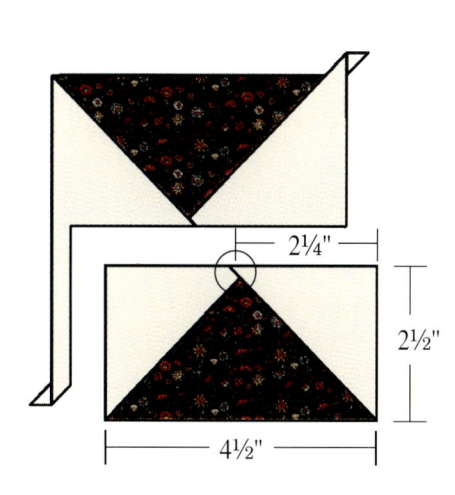

45

July

Making Four

1. Lay out patches in piles of four.
2. Flip right patch onto left patch. Match outside edges.
3. Sew across the point.
4. Assembly-line sew remaining pieces.
5. Press seam away from sewn point.
6. Square to 4 ½".

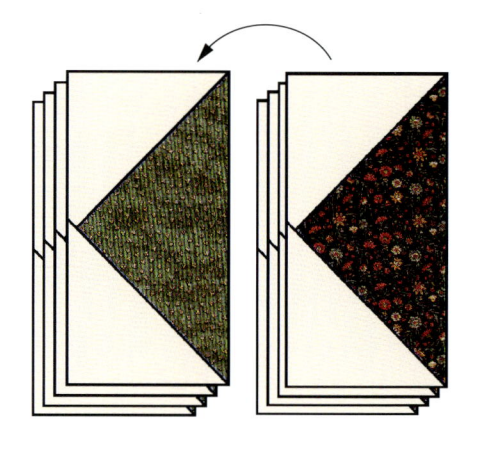

Making the Center

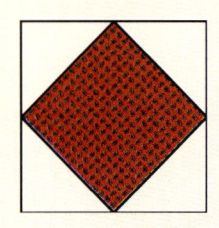

1. Lay out center square with light triangles.
2. Flip and pin opposite triangles onto square, allowing the triangle tips to show evenly. Sew with triangle on the bottom.
3. Press seams toward triangles.
4. Add remaining triangles.
5. Press seams toward triangles.
6. Square to 4 ½", centering points at 2 ¼". Leave ¼" seam allowance beyond points.

Sewing the Block Together

1. Lay out pieces.
2. Flip middle row onto left row, right sides together.
3. Assembly-line sew vertical seam.
4. Flip right row onto middle row. Sew.
5. Sew horizontal rows, pushing seams in opposite directions.
6. Press.

Twelve identical Illinois blocks use only three fabrics in distinctly light, medium and dark values. A black print frames the quilt and is repeated in the binding, while the main multi-colored dark fabric is the border. Without a lattice setting, the blocks form an overall pattern. The placement of the light values lets the emerging overall pattern float. "Stitch in the ditch" machine quilting with invisible thread is the finish.

The fabric used at the center of these four identical Illinois blocks is also at the block corners, forming a secondary pattern in combination with the lattice fabric. The lattice fabric is repeated as the dark fabric of the block and binding. The cornerstone fabric is picked up from the medium fabric of the block. The quilt is machine "stitched in the ditch" with invisible thread.

July

Sunday	Monday	Tuesday	Wednesday

Rockome Gardens
Barbara Gerichs, Controller
R. R. 2, Box 600
Arcola, IL 61910
(217) 268-4106

Barbara likes the Quilt in a Day *Quilters' Almanac* because she likes the variation of a sampler quilt.
Tip: Never store quilts in plastic bags. Air and refold quilts from time to time to prevent wear on the fold. (Barbara Gerichs)

July

Thursday	Friday	Saturday

Potato Doughnuts
Barbara Gerichs
Rockome Gardens

This recipe is from a cookbook entitled The Ladies Aid of the M.E. Church, Lerna, IL (c. 1900).

3 large potatoes, mashed smooth, or two cups mashed potatoes
butter, size of hickory nut
1 c. sugar
½ c. milk
1 egg
3 cs. flour
2 ½ t. baking powder
1 t. vanilla

Roll soft and fry in hot lard or beef drippings.

Devilled Ham Loaf with Mustard Sauce
Barbara Gerichs
Rockome Gardens

1-¼ pounds pork shoulder, ground
½ cup milk
1-¼ pounds smoked ham, ground
½ cup bouillon
¾ cup cracker crumbs
1 egg, slightly beaten
¼ t. Worcestershire Sauce
1 egg white, stiffly beaten

Combine all ingredients except egg white, mix thoroughly, fold in egg white, form into loaf, bake at 375° F., 1-½ hours.

Hot Mustard Sauce
¼ cup melted shortening
¼ cup sugar
2 T. flour
½ cup bouillon
¼ cup prepared mustard
1 egg yolk, well-beaten
⅓ cup lemon juice
¼ t. Worcestershire sauce

Combine shortening flour, bouillon, mustard, and sugar. Cook over hot water until thick and smooth. Add egg yolk, cook ten minutes. Add lemon juice and Worcestershire Sauce.

August

Salt Lake City

Suggested values: choose a light, a dark and three mediums.

Salt Lake City was founded in 1847 by Brigham Young and his Mormon followers. The city soon served as a supply depot for pioneers on their way to California.

Between the years of 1856 and 1860, ten handcart companies of nearly three thousand poor Mormon immigrants reached Salt Lake City. Priscilla Evans, one of the pioneers, pulled her hickory cart a total of 1330 miles from Iowa City, covering as much as fifteen miles a day.

Too poor to purchase necessary sewing supplies from occasional traveling peddlers, she improvised. She raveled a strip of shirting dyed with hickory for dark sewing thread.

Cutting Instructions

Layer cut right sides together:

(1) 4" x 8" rectangle light
(1) 4" x 8" rectangle dark

Cut:

(4) 2 ⅝" squares light

(2) 4 ¼" squares first medium
then cut on both diagonals

(4) 4" squares dark, then cut on diagonal

(2) 4" squares second medium, then cut on diagonal

(1) 4 ¾" square third medium or fussycut

To Make These Pieces

4

4

8

8

4

1

August

Making Four

1. Press rectangles right sides together.
2. Draw a 4" squaring line.
3. Method detail on page 7.
4. Press seam to light fabric.
5. Square to 3 ½".

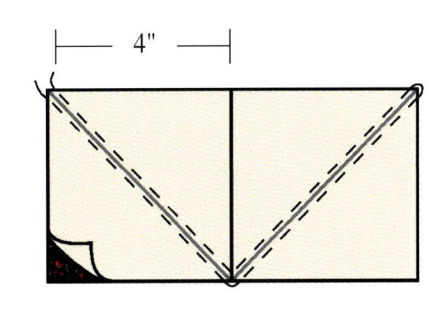

Making Four

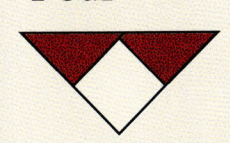

1. Stack four 2 ⅝" squares with 4 small triangles.
2. Flip square onto triangle matching top and right edges. Assembly-line sew.
3. Clip connecting threads. Fingerpress seam to triangle.

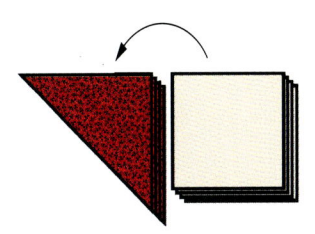

4. Stack sewn pieces with remaining triangles.
5. Flip triangle onto square matching top and right edges. Assembly-line sew.
6. Press seams to triangle. Trim exposed seam tips.

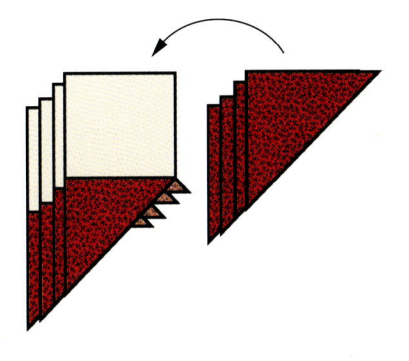

Making Four

1. Lay out sewn pieces and dark triangles in piles of four.
2. Fold and pinch a triangle to find mid-point of long edge. Right sides together, pin seam to mid-point of triangle.
3. Sew with solid triangle on the bottom.
4. Press seam toward solid triangle.

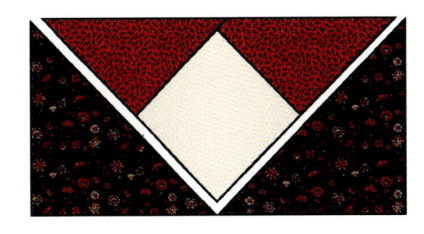

51

August

5. Repeat with remaining triangle.
6. Square each rectangle to 3 ½" x 6 ½", keeping ¼" seam allowance beyond points of square. Center points at 3 ¼".

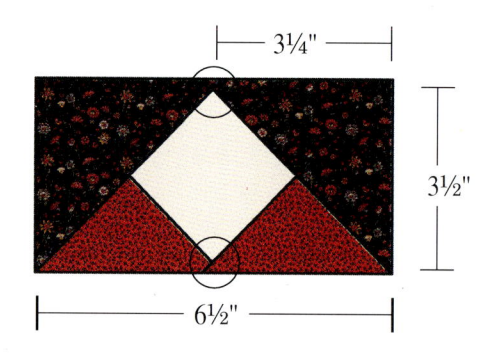

Making the Center

1. Lay out center square with medium triangles.
2. Flip and pin opposite triangles onto square allowing triangle tips to show evenly.
3. Sew with triangle on the bottom.
4. Press seams to triangles.
5. Add remaining triangles. Press seams to triangles.
6. Square to 6 ½" centering points at 3 ¼" on each side. Leave ¼" seam allowance beyond points.

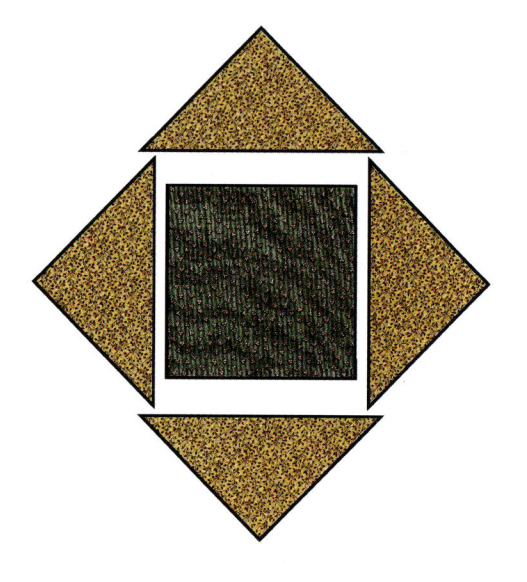

Sewing the Block Together

1. Lay out pieces.
2. Flip middle row onto left row, right sides together.
3. Assembly-line sew vertical seam.
4. Flip right row onto middle row. Sew.
5. Sew horizontal rows, pushing vertical seams in opposite directions.
6. Press.

The four identical Salt Lake City blocks set together with lattice and cornerstones are machine "stitched in the ditch" with invisible thread. The solid lattice picks up a color from the multi-colored main fabric in the blocks, while the cornerstones repeat the medium fabric. The binding is the main multi-colored fabric, and the lattice serves as a border.

The Salt Lake City block is unrecognizable when an overall pattern is planned. The four blocks are identical, but the values and colors are placed so as to contribute to a medallion look. The pattern is further hidden when two corners of each block are extended with a pieced border. A wide second border and the binding use the main multi-colored fabric. The quilting is machine "stitching in the ditch" with invisible thread.

August

August

Sunday	Monday	Tuesday	Wednesday

August

Gardiner's Sew & Quilt
Irene Gardiner
1508 Washington Blvd.
Ogden, UT 84404
(801) 394-4466

Irene says the *Quilt in a Day Log Cabin* has been her best selling book for 15 years. It's easy enough for people who have never made a quilt. They gain confidence.
Tip: It is much easier to straighten fabric after pre-washing.
(Irene Gardiner)

Thursday	Friday	Saturday

Salt Lake Bran Muffins

Irene Gardiner, Ogden, UT

This makes quite a few muffins depending on the size. The mixture can be stored up to 6 weeks in the refrigerator in a tightly covered container.

- 2 c. Nabisco 100% Bran
- 2 c. boiling water
- 3 c. white sugar
- 5 t. soda
- 1 c. vegetable shortening
- 1 t. salt
- 4 c. Kellogg's All Bran cereal (40% bran)
- 4 eggs
- 5 c. flour
- 1 qt. buttermilk
- 2 c. dates or raisins (optional)
- 1 c. nuts (optional)

Pour boiling water over the Nabisco 100% Bran (if using dates or raisins add at this time to soak). Cream shortening and sugar and add beaten eggs and milk; then add Kellogg's All Bran. Sift flour, soda, and salt, then add sifted dry ingredients to creamed shortening mixture. Fold in the soaked 100% Bran mixture. Bake in greased muffin tins, 18-20 min. at 400° F.

September

Arizona

Suggested values: choose a light, a dark and two mediums.

Arizona, gained through the Mexican War (1846–48) and the Gadsden Purchase (1853), was used as a transportation route to California.

A plucky woman called "Arizona Mary" earned a substantial livelihood driving a 16 yoke ox team, hauling supplies in the Southwest. Other women widowed on the trail continued westward, directing the family alone. Some found they could make as much as $100 a week doing men's laundry. Some became entrepreneurs, operating boarding houses for men far from family who longed for homecooking. Others became teachers, actresses, nurses, or missionaries.

Cutting Instructions

Layer cut right sides together:

(1) 6" square light
(1) 6" square dark

(1) 3" x 6" rectangle light
(1) 3" x 6" rectangle first medium

Cut:

(1) 5 ¼" square light
(1) 6 ½" square dark

(4) 2 ½" x 4 ½" rectangles first medium

(4) 2 ½" squares light

(1) 4 ½" square second medium or fussycut

To Make These Pieces

8

4

4

4

4

1

September

Making Eight and Four

1. Press 6" squares and 3" x 6" rectangles right sides together.
2. Draw squaring lines at 3".
3. Method detail on page 7.
4. Square to 2 ½".

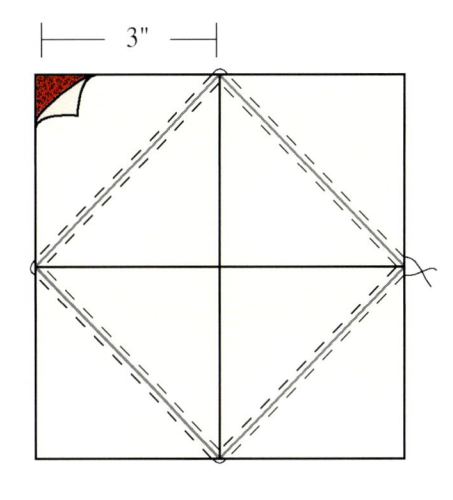

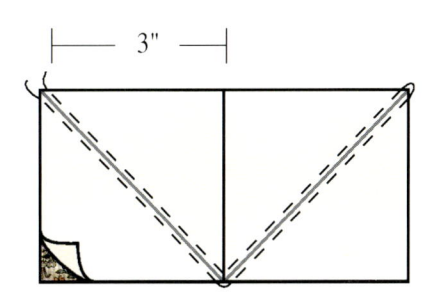

Making Four Units

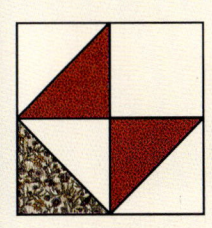

1. In piles of four, lay out 2 ½" corner squares with patches.
2. Flip right pieces onto left.
3. Assembly-line sew vertical seams.
4. Cut connecting thread between pairs.

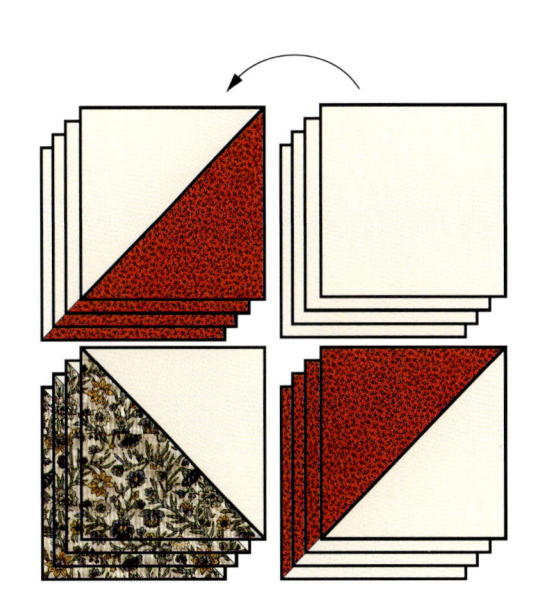

57

September

5. Sew horizontal seam, pushing seam toward darker fabric.

6. Press horizontal seam toward corner square.

7. Square to 4 ½".

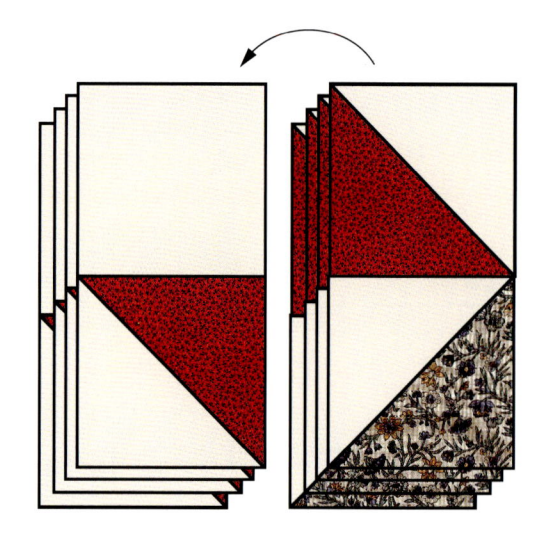

Making Four

1. Right sides together and same grain, center 5 ¼" square on 6 ½" square. Press.
2. Method detail on page 9.

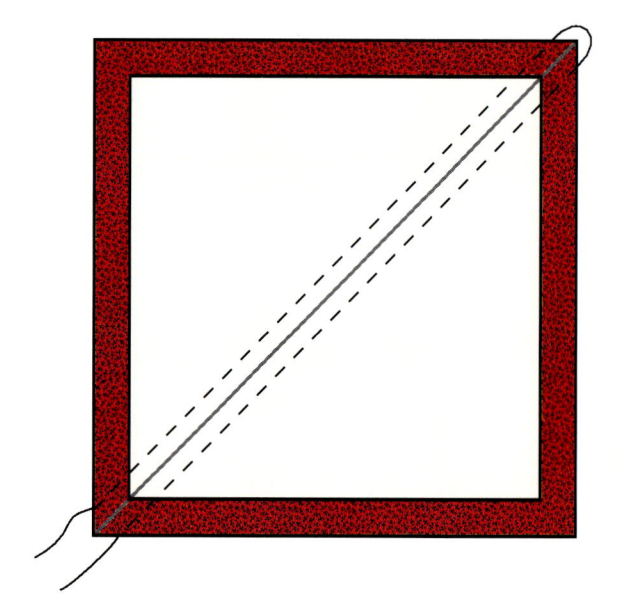

3. When trimming out four 2 ½" x 4 ½" patches, center peak at 2 ¼". Leave a ¼" seam allowance above peak. Seams end at bottom corners.

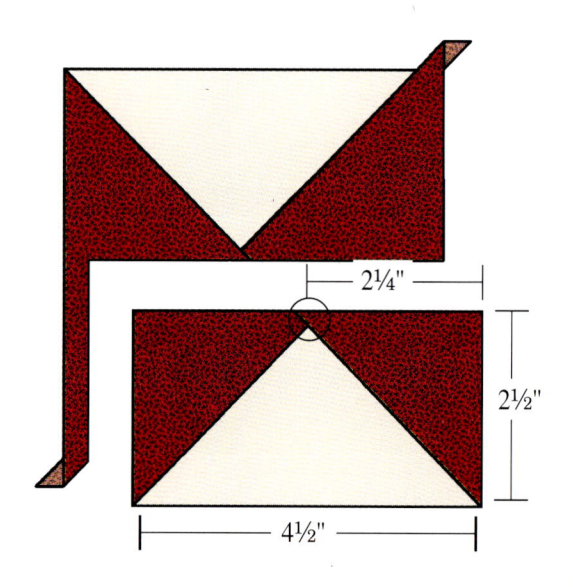

September

Making Four Units

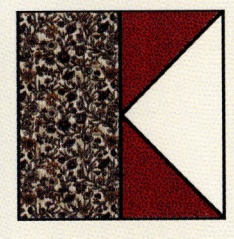

1. In piles of four, lay out rectangle patches with medium rectangles.
2. Flip right piece onto left. Match outside edges.
3. Sew across the peak. Assembly-line sew units.
4. Cut connecting threads. Press seam toward solid rectangle.
5. Square to 4 ½".

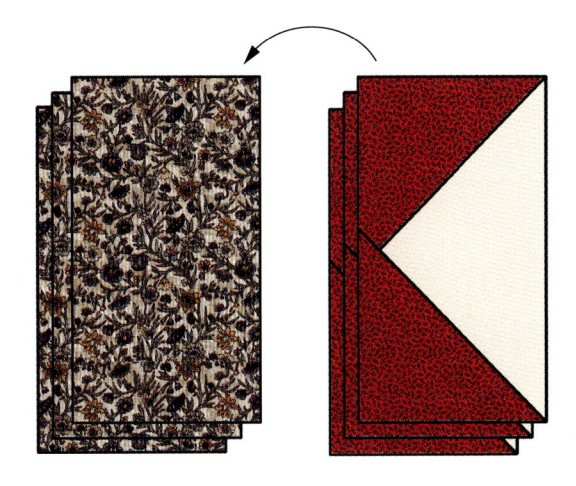

Sewing the Block Together

1. Lay out pieces.
2. Flip middle row onto left row, right sides together.
3. Assembly-line sew vertical seam.
4. Flip right row onto middle row. Sew.
5. Sew horizontal rows, pushing seams in opposite directions.
6. Press.

Arizona is the third block in the third row. Sew together the third row. Turn to the back of the Pioneer Sampler for instructions.

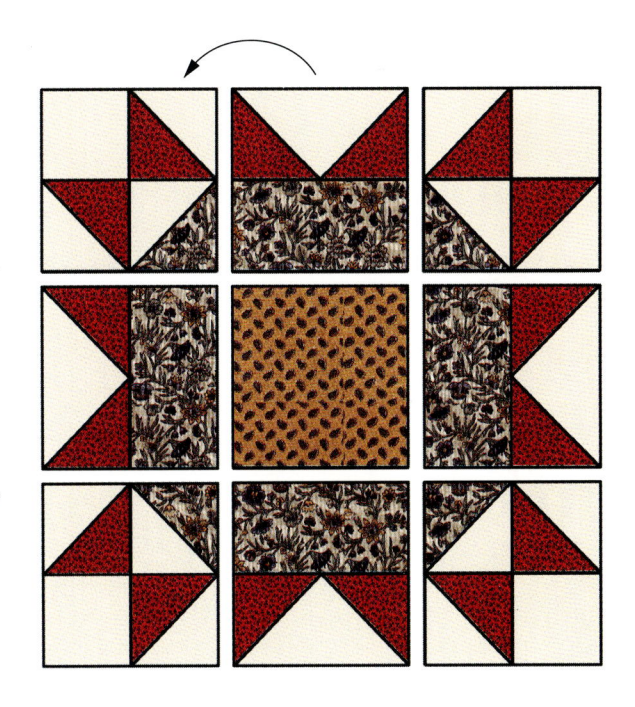

September

Sunday	Monday	Tuesday	Wednesd

September

The Quilt Basket, Inc
Peggy Peck
6538-C E. Tanque Verde Rd.
Tucson, AZ 85715
(602) 722-8810

Peggy likes all of the Quilt in a Day books. She especially likes *Dresden Plate* and says that it looks great in southwest colors.
Tip: Make a quilt, make a memory. Quilters in Arizona like to piece quilts in the winter, and quilt them in the summer when they stay indoors in the cool refrigeration of air-conditioning. (Peggy Peck)

Thursday	Friday	Saturday

Arizona Corn Bread

Peggy Peck, Tucson, AZ

1 box corn bread mix
1 small can whole kernel corn, drained
1 can green chili peppers, diced
Jack cheese

Mix cornbread according to directions. Place one-half of mixture into 8" square pan. Add drained corn in an even layer. Spread green chilies over corn. Arrange cheese slices over all, spread remaining corn bread mixture over top. Bake about 35 min. at 350° F.

October
Montana

Suggested values: choose a light, a dark and three mediums.

Gold discovered in 1858 at Goldcreek brought settlers with their colorful stories of fortunes made and lost overnight, of murderous groups preying on stage coaches, of corrupt sheriffs and vigilante groups.

Rachel Bond and her young husband, Allen, joined her uncle's wagon train in 1853 with only a bundle of fabric scraps. Without supplies, Rachel was grateful to find an old copper kettle along the road. As she walked westward sewing her squares, she stored her quilt pieces in the kettle draped over her arm. Rachel and Allen agreed at the end of the trail, arriving with only a kettle and a quilt, all was worthwhile.

Cutting Instructions

Layer cut right sides together:

(1) 5" x 10" rectangle light
(1) 5" x 10" rectangle dark

(1) 1 ⅞" x 21" strip first medium
(1) 1 ⅞" x 21" strip second medium

Cut:

(4) 1 ⅞" x 4 ⅞" rectangles dark
(8) 2" x 3" rectangles light

(1) 1 ⅞" x 4 ½" strip light
(2) 1 ⅞" x 4 ½" strips third medium

(2) 1 ⅞" squares light
(1) 1 ⅞" square third medium

To Make These Pieces

4

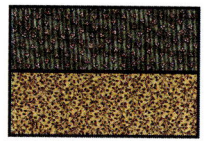

4

4

2

1

October

Making Four

1. Press rectangles right sides together.
2. Draw a 5" squaring line.
3. Method details on page 7.
4. Square to 4 ½".

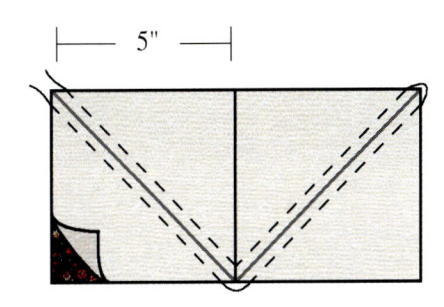

Making Four

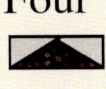

1. Fold each 1 ⅞" x 4 ⅞" dark piece lengthwise in half to find center. Press a crease.
2. On wrong side, mark a dot at center crease, ¼" from top edge.
3. Draw sewing lines from lower corners through dot to top edge.

4. Right sides together, lay marked piece on a 2" x 3" light piece so its marked line runs diagonally corner to corner on light piece. Pin.
5. Hold threads and sew on drawn line. Assembly-line sew remaining pieces. Lay ruler's ¼" line on stitching and trim excess.

6. Press seam allowance away from center.

7. Repeat with other side, sewing from the corner toward the dot. Extend the drawn line for easier corner to corner matching.

8. Do not "square up" these pieces.

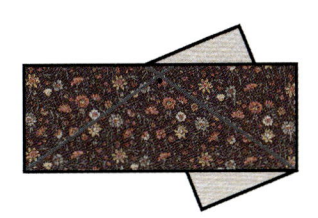

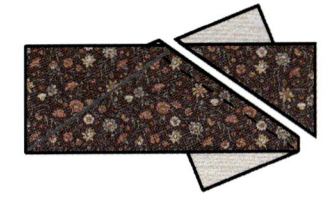

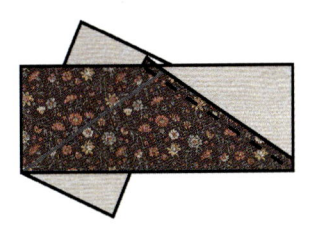

Making Four

1. Sew 21" medium strips right sides together.
2. Press seams toward second medium.
3. Sew patches to first medium side of strip, leaving about ¼" between patches.
4. Press seams toward strip. Cut apart.
5. Square evenly to 4 ½" with peak centered at 2 ¼". Leave ¼" seam allowance beyond peak and at side points.

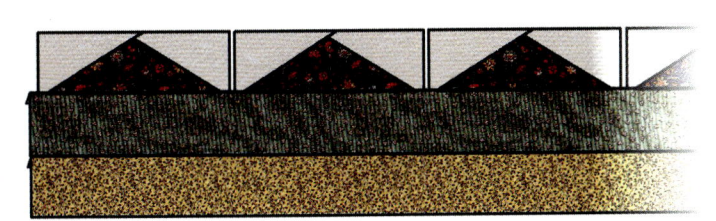

63

October

Making the Center

1. Lay out light 4 ½" strip between medium strips.
2. Sew three strips together.
3. Press seams toward medium fabric.
4. Trim left end. Cut two 1 ⅞" pieces.

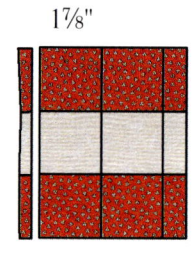

1⅞"

5. Lay out medium square between light squares and sew together. Press seams toward medium.

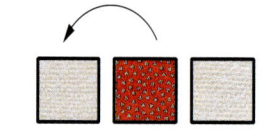

6. Lay out three pieced strips. Sew together wiggle matching seams. Press seams away from center.

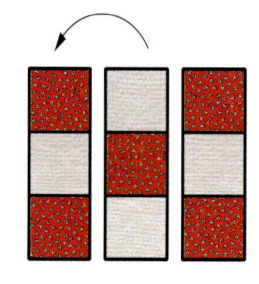

7. Square evenly to 4 ½".

Sewing the Block Together

1. Lay out pieces.
2. Flip middle row onto left row, right sides together.
3. Assembly-line sew vertical seam.
4. Flip right row onto middle row. Sew.
5. Sew horizontal rows, pushing seams in opposite directions.
6. Press.

The main multi-colored fabric at the center of these four identical Arizona blocks is repeated in the lattice for a busy look. The medium fabric is used in the blocks and cornerstones, while the dark fabric is seen in the dark points of the block and binding. The quilt is machine quilted by "stitching the ditch" with invisible thread.

These four Montana blocks in busy fabrics are separated with a wide, solid lattice and cornerstones of the darkest fabric. The main multi-colored floral print is repeated in the binding. The patches and block seams are machine quilted with invisible thread by "stitching in the ditch."

Soften chapped, windburn skin with buttermilk and cornstarch.
Anonymous 1889

Scent your clothing overnight by tying a sachet of roses to the inside of your dress.
Anonymous 1877

65

October

Sunday	Monday	Tuesday	Wednesday

October

Patchworks
Margo Krager
126 E. Main St.
Bozeman, MT 59715
(406) 587-2112

Margo says that she likes the Depression Era fabrics. *Sunbonnet Sue* is a wonderful way to show off a collection of 1930's prints.
Tip: When choosing fabrics for a quilting project, include fabric designs that vary in scale and texture. Remember that the finished product will not be viewed from a few inches away, and large scale florals, geometrics, and textural prints can be combined to produce a visually exciting quilt. (Margo Krager)

Thursday	Friday	Saturday

Calico Potatoes

Margo Krager, Bozeman, MT

raw diced potatoes *(one per person)*
chopped green onions
cubed Velvetta cheese (regular or Mexican)
buttermilk
salt & pepper

Toss potatoes, onions and cheese together. Sprinkle with salt and pepper. Place in 2 quart greased casserole and pour in a small amount of buttermilk. Cover and bake at 350° 1 to 1 ½ hours.

November

Missouri Star

Suggested values: choose a light, a dark and two mediums.

Missouri served as a springboard for countless westward-bound settlers. Pioneers were not to leave St. Louis, "Gateway to the West," without the best map available. "The Emigrants' Guide to California" recommended two or three quilts per traveler, valued at a whopping $22.50!

The outdoor experience of the overland journey inspired women to use nature in quilt patterns, as in this star. Diamond stars also had a migration theme with reference to divine guidance.

Cutting Instructions

Layer cut right sides together:

(1) 4 ½" x 9" rectangle dark
(1) 4 ½" x 9" rectangle first medium

Cut:

(1) 7 ¼" square light
then cut on both diagonals

(4) 3 ½" squares light

(2) 4" squares dark, then cut on diagonal

(1) 4 ¾" square second medium or fussycut

To Make These Pieces

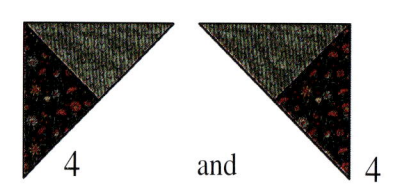

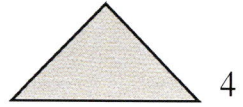

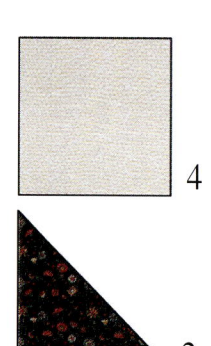

4   and   4

4

4

2

1

November

Making Four and Four

1. Press 4 ½" x 9" rectangles right sides together.
2. Draw a 4 ½" squaring line.
3. Draw diagonal lines. Pin.
4. Sew ¼" on both sides of diagonal lines. Press.
5. Cut on drawn lines.

6. Press seams toward darker fabric.
7. Be sure seams end at corners when squaring to 3 ⅞". *It's easier to square to 4", then to 3 ⅞".*

8. Cut on diagonal across seam. Do not press this bias edge.

Making Four

1. In piles of four, lay out light triangles with pieced triangles, darker tip to base of light triangle.

2. Flip a pieced triangle onto light triangle. Match bottom edge of light triangle with dark triangle. Pin and sew a ¼" seam down to bottom edge.

3. Press seam toward pieced triangle. Do not touch iron to bias cut edge.

November

4. In the same manner, add the opposite triangle.

5. Carefully trim patch to 3 ½" x 6 ½", with peak centered at 3 ¼" and seams ending at corners. Leave ¼" seam allowance above peak.

Making the Center

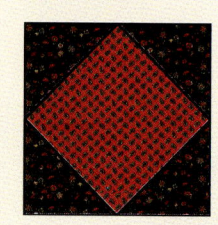

1. Lay out Center square with dark triangles.
2. Flip and pin opposite triangles onto square with triangle tips showing evenly. Sew with triangle on bottom.
3. Press seams toward triangles.
4. Add remaining triangles, and press seams toward triangles.
5. Square to 6 ½" square, centering points at 3 ¼". Leave a ¼" seam allowance beyond points.

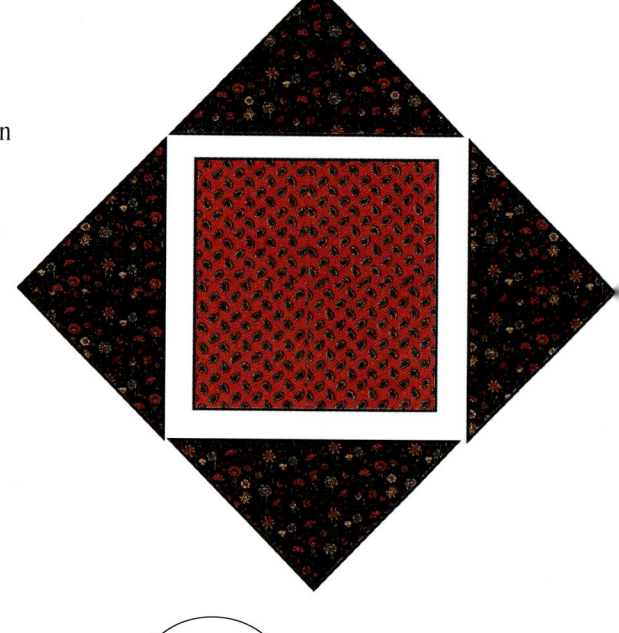

Sewing the Block Together

1. Lay out pieces.
2. Flip middle row onto left row, right sides together.
3. Assembly-line sew vertical seam.
4. Flip right row onto middle row. Sew.
5. Sew horizontal rows, pushing seams in opposite directions.
6. Press.

Four Missouri Stars feature a main multi-colored floral fabric at the center of each block, in the border, and in the binding. The lattice-without-cornerstones is the same dark print as the points of the star. Machine "stitching in the ditch" with invisible thread finishes the quilt.

The Missing Needle

The year was 1853 and Grandmother Drain owned the only darning needle in Pass Creek Canyon, Oregon. It was the most cared-for-possession in the small community of fifteen families! When clothing needed to be patched and mended, everyone knew Grandmother Drain would lend it out.

Sharing the needle went well—until the day eight year old Jimmy Chitwood was to take it back to its owner. Mrs. Chitwood put a long red raveling through the eye of the needle, knotted the raveling, put the needle into a potato, and sent Jimmy off to Grandmother Drain's cabin.

The small animals on the trail did not distract Jimmy from his important mission—until a mother bear with her two cubs came into sight! He quickly hid behind a stump under a bush until the bears left, and then he went on. Oh, yes, as you guessed! The worst happened to poor Jimmy! Imagine his horror to discover the only needle in town was lost while under his care.

All of the neighbors joined in the search—a search which seemed futile. Suddenly Jimmy disappeared into the bushes. When he reappeared, he had the needle—still stuck in the potato. Jimmy had finally recalled the stump where he had hidden when frightened by the bears. The whole town shared in the joy of finding the needle.

One day in the fall of 1855, the head of the needle broke off as Grandmother Drain was sewing. All of the ladies in Pass Creek Canyon hoped that a needle would soon be provided.

It was around Thanksgiving when a peddler rode into Pass Creek on a mule. One of the ladies bought a comb, two bought dress goods, another one bought a doll head. Then, they remembered the need for a needle, and shared their story. Being a generous man, the peddler gave a "Christmas present" to each of the families of Pass Creek Canyon.

The peddler was Aaron Meier. After several years of peddling his wares across Oregon he opened his own store in Portland in 1857. With the help of his family, he developed the Meier and Frank Company into one of America's great family-owned department stores.

The Oregonian ran a full-page ad on January 1, 1967. The headline read "Have you ever heard the story of 'The Potato and the Darning Needle'?" At the end was an invitation: "We still want every woman to have a darning needle of her own. Come into our Fabric Center at any one of our three stores Tuesday and get yours, free."

Pioneer folklore from Women's Voices from the Oregon Train, pp. 134-135
Susan G. Butruille, Tamarack Books, Inc., Boise, ID, 1993

November

Sunday	Monday	Tuesday	Wednesday

November

Marlys Michaelson, Owner
Quilts & Quilts Country Store
1137 W. Highway 76
Branson Hts. Shopping Ctr.
Branson, MO 65616
417\334-3243

Marlys says that the Quilt in a Day *Log Cabin* and *Sunbonnet Sue* are her favorites. However, the shop stocks a lot of Quilt in a Day books because they are all very popular. Quilts & Quilts specializes in coordinating fabrics to meet quilters' special requests.

Tip: You will feel better and be able to sew or quilt longer if you get up at least once an hour to stretch and walk around.

Thursday	Friday	Saturday

Chicken n' Dressing

Darlene Palmer
El Cajon, CA

2 chickens, stewed & boned
8-9 cups crumbled corn bread
3-4 slices of bread
1 ¼ cup chopped onions
¾ t. pepper
1 t. salt (or to taste)
2T. ground sage
3 eggs
celery (optional)

Combine all of the ingredients except the chicken. Pour 5-6 cups chicken broth over above and mix well with potato masher to a thick batter consistency. Mix the ingredients right into the baking pan. After mixing, press the chicken pieces into the mixture, almost covering the chicken. Add a little more broth to the top. Bake at 400° F. about 45 minutes to 1 hour until brown or set. Serve with giblet gravy.

Eleanor Burns will be appearing at Quilt Festival, George R. Brown Convention Center, Houston, TX, November 3-6.

December
Kentucky Chain

Suggested values: choose a light, a dark and a mediums.

Kentucky, meaning "prairie," was an Indian hunting ground. Once Cumberland Gap was discovered in 1750, countless explorers and settlers moved through it. One of the best known explorers was the legendary Daniel Boone.

As the Jacob Robbins family, natives of Kentucky, traveled westward, they experienced bad weather, swarms of bugs, insufficient food, and bad water. The water may have caused cholera, a highly infectious illness, resulting in the deaths of three of his daughters. The girls were buried together in a wagon box, covered with quilts.

Cutting Instructions

Cut:

(4) 4 ¼" squares light,
    then cut on diagonals

Layer cut:

(1) 2 ¾" x 36" strip medium
(1) 2 ¾" x 36" strip dark

    then cut each strip into:
    (4) 2 ¾" x 4" pieces

    and
    (2) 2 ¾" x 9 ½" strips

To Make These Pieces

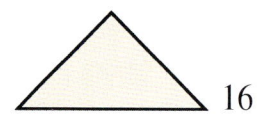

16

4

4

2

2

December

Making Four and Four

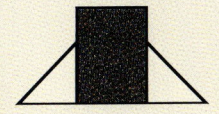

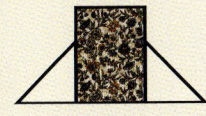

1. In piles of eight, lay out triangles with 4" dark and medium pieces.

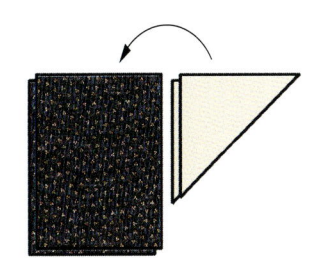

2. Flip a triangle onto 4" piece, right sides together, matching top edges. Assembly-line sew.

3. Repeat, sewing remaining eight triangles to other side of pieces.
4. Press seams toward triangles. Avoid touching iron to unsewn bias edge.

Making Two and

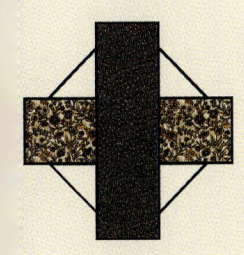

1. In piles of two lay dark patches with medium 9 ½" strips.

2. Press center folds on strip's length and width. Mark edges.

3. Press center fold along length of pieced patch. Mark edges.

4. Flip 9 ½" strip onto left patch, matching creases. Pin. Sew.

75

December

Two

5. Flip and sew right side.

6. Repeat with medium patches and dark strips.

7. Press seams toward triangles.

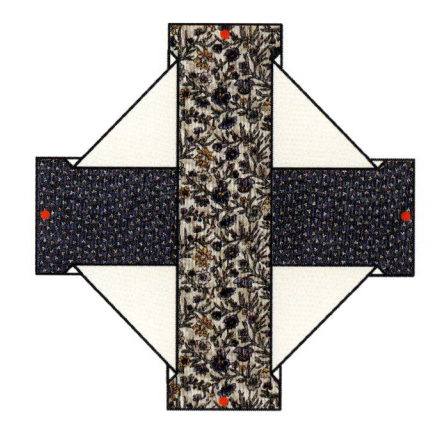

Trimming Quarters

1. Lay a Quarter on cutting mat with vertical and horizontal marked edges on grid lines.

2. Lay a Square Up ruler's diagonal line on center vertical line. Move ruler until its top point rests on marked fabric and its 6 ½" lines are on horizontal marked edges. Trim two upper sides.

3. Turn block around and trim, squaring to 6 ½".

4. Repeat with remaining Quarters.

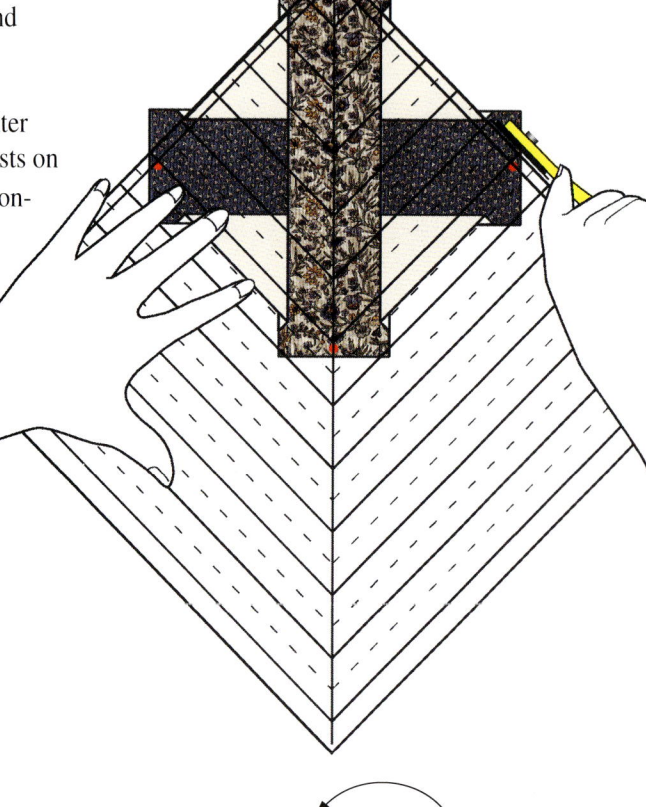

Sewing the Block Together

1. Lay out Quarters.
2. Flip right pieces onto left.
3. Assembly-line sew vertical seam.
4. Sew horizontal rows, pushing vertical seams in opposite directions.
5. Press.

Kentucky Chain is the third block in the fourth row. Sew together the fourth row. Turn to the back of the book for instructions.

Nine Kentucky Chain blocks show the weaving effect in an overall pattern. The dark and medium values of the "chain" fabrics give dimension to the quilt, and the dark fabric is used in the border and binding. While the method presented is fast and efficient for one block, a strip method for constructing several blocks for an overall pattern would be a more practical approach. The quilt is "stitched in the ditch" with invisible thread.

To seal the cracks of the wagon against water, carry a bucket of tar, and apply liberally.
Great Platte River
1843

Pack fresh eggs in oats and they will last several weeks.
Jerome Dickson
May, 1864

December

Sunday	Monday	Tuesday	Wednesday

Donna's Stitchery Nook
Donna Stuerzenberger
2845 W. Parrish Ave., Ste F
Owensboro, KY 42301
(502) 685-0404

Donna likes Quilt in a Day *Lover's Knot* because it is her husband's favorite. She made his in Americana colors.

Tip: Remember to press, NOT iron. (Donna Stuerzenberger)

December

Thursday	Friday	Saturday

Kentucky Salad

Roslyn Payne, Oceanside, CA

2 pkgs. lime gelatin dessert
2 c. crushed pineapple, drained
1 ½ c. grated cucumber, drained
1 t. lemon juice
1 c. cold water
pineapple juice and water to make
2 cs. very hot liquid

Drain pineapple and cucumber well, reserving pineapple juice. Make gelatin dessert according to package recipe, using 1 cup cold water and the reserved pineapple juice and water for the 2 cups of hot liquid. Chill to consistency of egg white. Fold in pineapple, cucumber, and lemon juice. Pour into mold and refrigerate. Unmold and serve on crisp lettuce with mayonnaise. (This is so cool on a hot day.)

Candied Sweet Potatoes Kentucky Style

Roslyn Payne, Oceanside, CA

6 medium sweet potatoes
(cut in half)
¾ c. water
2 c. brown sugar
4 T. melted butter
¼ c. broken pecans or walnuts

Put water, sugar and butter in a casserole on a very low heat to simmer. Peel and boil potatoes. When tender, transfer them to the syrup and add nuts. Bake in moderate over, 300°F. for 30 mins. Serves 6 to 8.

Finishing Your Quilt

Choose one method of finishing your quilt.
- Quick Turn and Tie Finish
- Machine Quilted Finish

Checking Your Blocks

If any of the match points need improving, "unsew" with your rotary cutter. Hold it between the thumb and forefinger of your right hand and support it with your middle finger. Drop the blade against the stitches as you put tension on the two pieces of fabric, exposing the seam. Resew.

Check that each block is approximately 12 ½" square. Straighten the outside edges if necessary without trimming away any of the ¼" seam allowance.

Do not be concerned if there is a slight variance in block sizes. If the blocks average slightly less than 12 ½", trim the 12 ½" lattice pieces to that measurement.

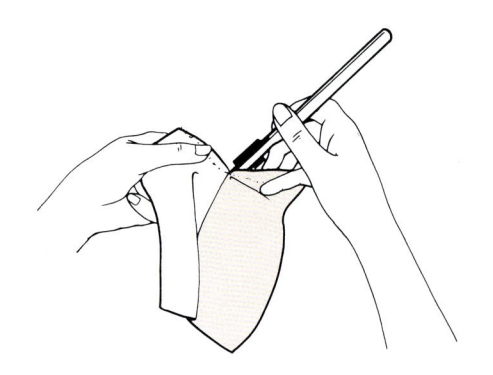

Quick Turn and Tie Finish

Use this method if you are not going to machine quilt each individual block. Lay out the blocks in rows quarterly, or arrange to suit your taste. Sew three blocks into rows.

Sewing the Unquilted Blocks Together

1. Lay out rows of blocks with 12 ½" lattice between them.

2. Sew together, stretching or easing each block to fit the lattice as you stitch.

3. Measure a row of sewn together blocks. Trim (5) 45" lattice strips to that measurement.

4. Pin and sew a long lattice strip to the top of each sewn together row.

5. So that rows line up, extend lines from the 12 ½" lattice strips and chalk mark on the long strips.

6. Pin-match the marked lattice to the lower edge of each row, and sew the rows together.

7. Piece the four remaining 45" lattice strips into two long strips. Measure, pin and sew to the two long sides of the quilt.

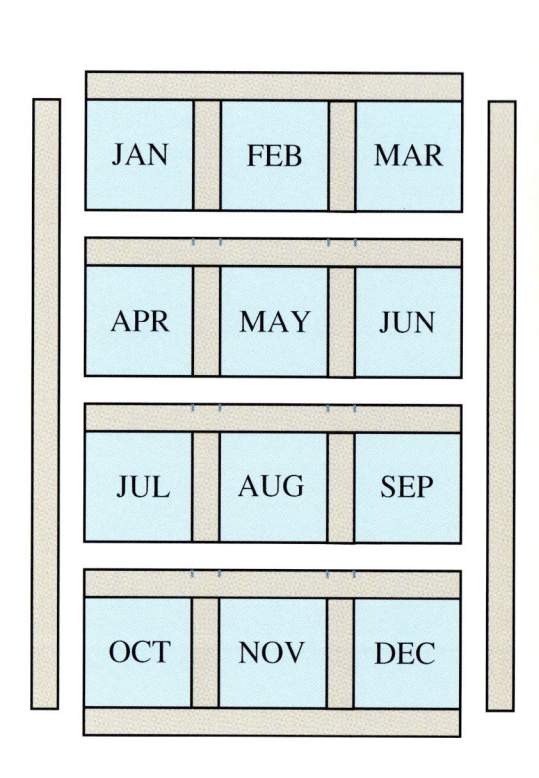

Finishing Your Quilt

Seminole Patchwork (optional)

Making Four Corners

1. Press rectangles right sides together.
2. Draw a 4" squaring line.
3. Draw diagonal lines. Pin.
4. Sew a ¼" on both sides of diagonal lines. Press.
5. Cut on drawn lines.
6. Press seams to darker fabric.
7. Set aside.

Making Seventy Eight

1. Stack up 2 ½" strips in this color order:

    lattice   medium   border

    Place 5 strips in each stack.
2. Assembly-line sew strips together lengthwise.
3. Press seams toward center.
4. Layer several sets of strips on cutting mat. Square the left end.
5. Layer cut (78) 2 ½" pieces. 
6. Set two pieces aside. 
7. Divide the remainder into two equal piles with 38 in each. Place so that second piece is one step lower than previous piece.

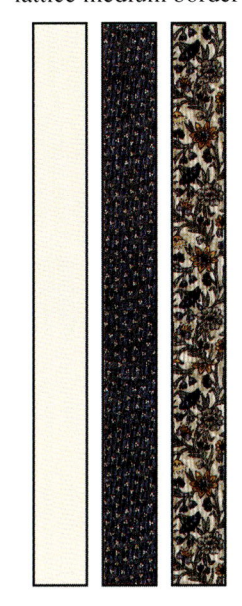

lattice medium border

Finishing Your Quilt

8. Flip second piece right sides together to first. The lattice fabric on top piece should extend up over medium seam by ¼".

9. Match and fingerpin the seams.

10. Stitch to the end.

11. Assembly-line sew all pairs.

12. Clip threads holding them together.

13. Set two pairs aside. Stack remainder into two piles.

14. Assembly-line sew pairs together into groups of four, making certain each new piece is one step lower than the previous one.

15. Sew two long pieces with 17 segments in each. (four sets of four plus one piece set aside.)

16. Sew two more long pieces with 22 segments in each. (five sets of four plus one pair set aside.)

17. Press flat.

Finishing Your Quilt

18. Line up the ¼" line on 6" x 24" ruler with medium points on seminole. Trim off tips of the seminole strip.

19. Measure the width of the trimmed strip. It should be approximately 3 ½" wide. **Square the four corner squares to that measurement.**

20. Square off each end ¼" from center, allowing for the ¼" seam allowance.

Square off ¼" from center.

21. Pin the piece with 17 segments right sides together to the two short sides of the quilt, through all thicknesses. Ease if necessary. *If there is too much to ease, take a deeper seam allowance on several segments until the strip fits.*

22. Sew through all thicknesses. Flip out, and finger press flat.

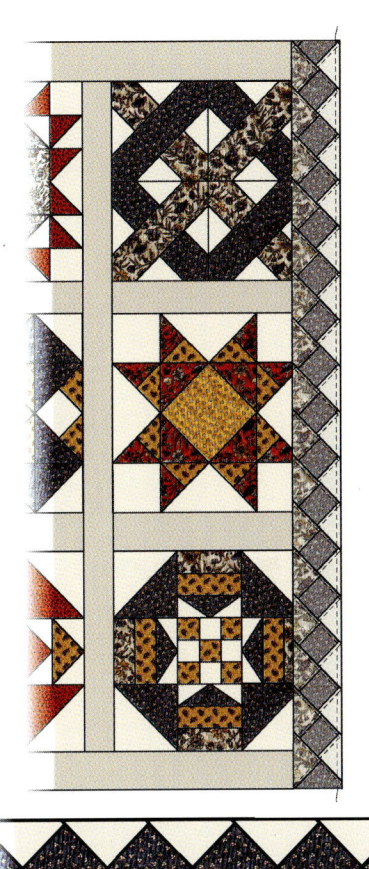

23. Sew the four corner squares to the ends of the two long strips. Carefully match the points.

24. Pin, ease, and sew the two remaining seminole sides to the quilt.

83

Finishing Your Quilt

Sewing the Borders to the Unquilted Top

1. Measure the width of the quilt. Cut two equal pieces.
2. Pin and stitch to the top and bottom.
3. Unfold, and measure the length, including the two borders.
4. Pin and sew the side borders.

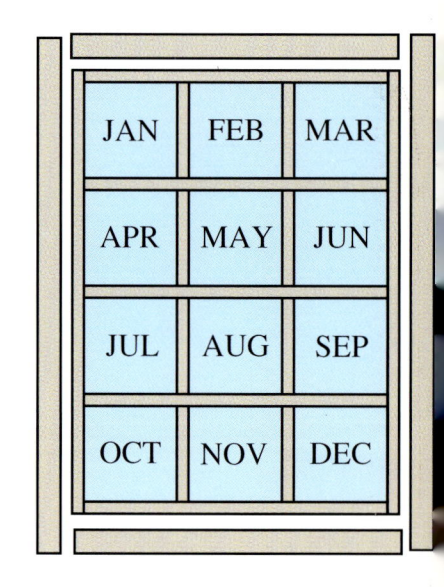

JAN	FEB	MAR
APR	MAY	JUN
JUL	AUG	SEP
OCT	NOV	DEC

Example of Colorado quilt

Quick Turning the Unquilted Top

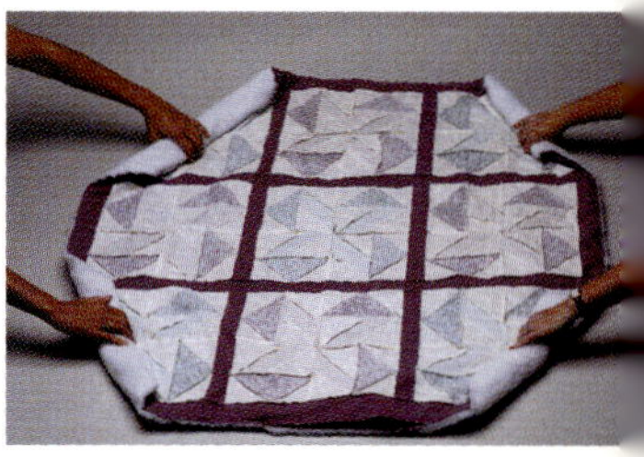

1. Place the quilt right sides together to the backing.
2. Pin around the outside edge. Trim the excess backing.
3. Stitch around the outside edge, leaving a 15" opening in the middle of one side. Do not turn right side out.
4. Lay the bonded batting out flat. Place the quilt on top.

    Trim excess batting. Loosely stitch the layers together to the seam allowance.

5. Station a person at each corner of the quilt. Begin rolling tightly in each corner and the sides toward the opening.

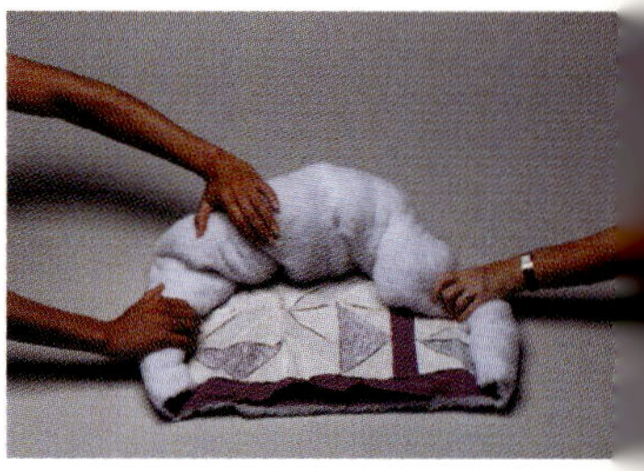

6. Open up the opening over this wad of fabric and batting, pop the quilt right side out through the hole, and carefully unroll with the layers together.

7. Working on opposite sides, grasp the edges of the quilt and pull in opposite directions to smooth out the batting.
8. Whipstitch the opening shut.

9. Tie surgeon's square knots at the corners of each block with a curved needle and embroidery floss.

Finishing Your Quilt

Machine Quilted Finish

Use this method if you are going to machine quilt blocks on rows of batting. Three blocks are machine quilted, quarterly if you'd like.

Cutting the Piece of Lightweight Bonded Batting

Machine Quilting Blocks in Rows to Batting

1. Cut the batting to the exact size of 63" x 81".

2. Leave the lightweight bonded batting in one large piece and cut off each row of batting as you need it.

1. Place the February block on the 25" strip of batting in bottom center position. Let the edge of the block hang over ¼". Pin in place. To manage the batting, roll the edges and safety pin in place.

2. Thread your machine with invisible thread. Loosen your top tension, and lengthen your stitch to 8-10 stitches per inch. Use walking foot.

3. Load your bobbin with neutral sewing thread.

4. Decide what pieces of the block to outline. "Stitch in the ditch" by placing the needle in the depth of the seam, and stitch. Backstitch. You may "machine quilt" by lining up the presser foot with the edge of the pieces, and stitch ¼" away from the seam.

   If possible, stitch continuously without removing the block from under the needle. Pivot with the needle in the fabric at the points.

5. Pin a 12 ½" lattice right sides together to each side of the block. Stitch through all thicknesses, and fold back.

6. Pin the January and March blocks right sides together to each lattice. Stitch, fold back and pin. "Stitch in the ditch, or machine quilt."

7. Measure the three blocks. Trim (5) 45" lattice strips to that measurement.

8. Sew a long lattice strip to the top of the row. The first three rows are sewn in this manner.

9. On the bottom row, long lattice strips are sewn to the top and bottom of the blocks. To allow room for the top along lattice strip, position the center block 2 ½" down from the top of the batting.

The four rows of blocks quilted to the batting are now sewn together into one top.

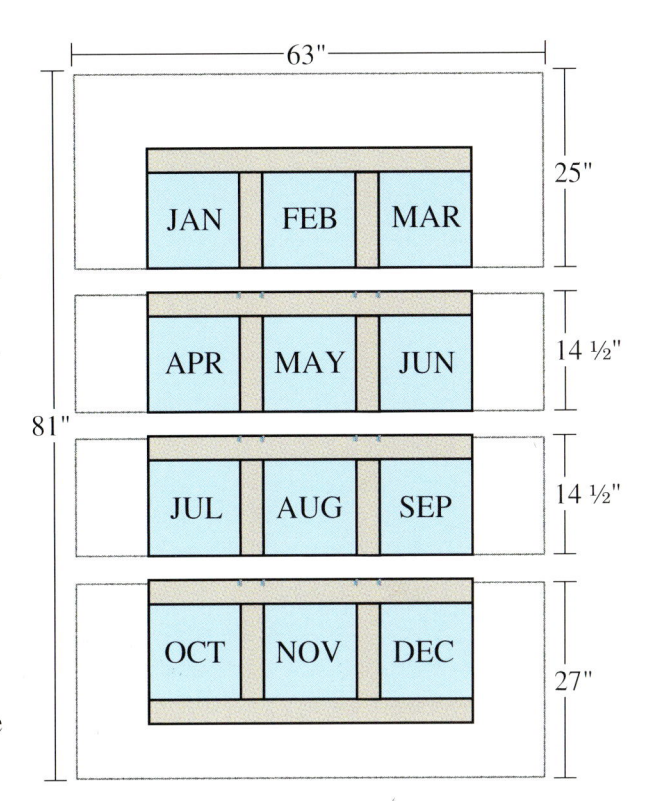

Machine quilt ¼" from seam.

"Stitch in the ditch"

85

Finishing Your Quilt

Sewing the Machine Quilted Rows Together

1. So that rows line up, extend lines from the 12 ½" lattice strips and chalk mark on the long strips.

2. Place the second row right sides together to the first row. If necessary, snip the batting away from the edges, and fold back out of the way.

3. Match-pin the lattice. Stretch or ease each lattice to fit each block as you stitch.

4. Fold the two rows back and flat. Trim away any excess batting, and pat flat. Hand whipstitch the butted batting.

5. Add the remaining two rows in this manner.

Layering the Quilted Top on the Backing

1. Spread out the backing on a large table or floor area with the right side down. Clamp the fabric to the edge of the table with binder clips or tape the backing to the floor.

2. With the top right side up, center on the backing. Smooth until all layers are flat.

3. Safety pin the layers together through the lattice. Use a grapefruit spoon or pinning tool to assist the process.

4. Piece the remaining lattice strips. Measure the sides, and cut the lattice that measurement.

5. Pin the lattice right sides together to the sides through all thicknesses.

6. Stitch, using 10 stitches per inch, bobbin thread to match the backing, and a walking foot.

7. Unfold both long lattice back and flat. Pin.

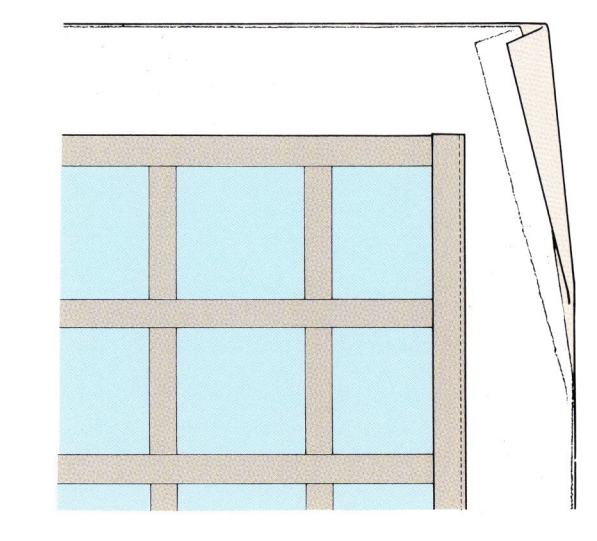

Adding Seminole (optional)

Refer to page 81.

Pin and sew through all thicknesses.

Sewing the Borders

1. Measure the width of the quilt. Cut two equal pieces.

2. Pin and stitch to the top and bottom through all thicknesses.

3. Unfold, and measure the length, including the two borders.

4. Pin and sew the side borders.